Floral Fantasies

by Lennie Honcoop

Acknowledgements

Author, quilt designer
Lennie Honcoop
Dutch Quilter
Elk Grove, California

Illustrator, book designer
Anita Hallock
Fast Patch
Springfield, Oregon

Photographer
Jeremy Cloud
Cloud Photography
Modesto, California

Editor
Gary Honcoop
Dutch Quilter's "Silent Partner"

Machine quilter
Julie Gutierrez
Quilter's Paradise
Anderson, California

Printer
Palmer Printing
St. Cloud, Minnesota

Publisher
Dutch Quilter
4105 Saul Court
Elk Grove, California

Thanks

A big thank you to my friends, students, and fellow quilters who bought my first book, *Oregon Coast Lighthouses.* Their enthusiasm and support inspired me to design this new set of patterns and write a second book.

Contents

Flowers – I love them!

I think one of the reasons I love flowers is that I lived for the first 25 years of my life in The Netherlands – the land of tulips. I recall as a child my excitement when I would find the first flowers in bloom each spring, often crocuses peeking through a layer of snow. Even now I experience a twinge of homesickness when I see pictures of the tulips field and the stunning display of flowers in Keukenhof – the largest display of bulb flowers in the world. The tulip fields that extend for mile after mile with alternating strips of colors look like the world's largest flower quilt.

So, it was really not a difficult choice when I began thinking about the theme for a second book of applique patterns. The range of colors and shapes of flowers is so great that I had more subjects for patterns than I could possible hope to design. One of the more enjoyable aspects of designing patterns for this book was poring over the hundreds of flower pictures and finding those special ones that I wanted to feature.

I believe God created the vast array of flowers to provide beautiful exclamation points in His creation. I hope I can help you capture some of that beauty through these patterns and that you will enjoy creating your own floral fantasies!

Lennie

Dedication

To my husband Gary and boys, Alex and Nathan, with gratitude for your support and willingness to put up with me during my preoccupation with getting the book finished. Thanks much—and I love you!

My way of doing appliqué

I'm not fond of tedious hand stitching or satin stitching. That's why I love this easy no-sew appliqué method. I just finish edges with Hot Ribbon!

1. Trace the pattern pieces on Steam-a-Seam2.

Place the sheet over the page. It doesn't matter which side is down. Copy any numbers or other marks too.

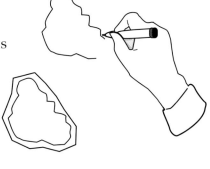

2. Cut the pieces out roughly.

Leave at least 1/8" of fusible material around each shape.

3. Remove the backing paper and press the pieces to the back of the fabric.

Take your time and find just the right spots to use for the large and important pieces. (See page 11.)

> *Darker areas:* Use them for parts of the petals near the center of the flower, or for leaves which are back in the shadows.
>
> *Streaks:* Decide which direction streaks would go on a real leaf or petal, and take advantage of any streaks in the fabric.

Wrong side of fabric

Although you might need a warm iron to press the pieces in place, you can probably just finger press them. That's one reason I like Steam-a-Seam2.

4. Cut out the pieces carefully.

Leave the paper on for now.

Tip: If you won't get to Step 6 right away, keep pieces sorted in bags or envelopes to avoid losing any.

Leaves

5. Make a large copy of the placement guide.

Use a photocopier to enlarge the placement guides, usually on 11" x 17" paper. If some of the diagram is missing from the enlargement, that's okay, but try to include part of each flower or leaf.

If necessary, you can copy half the diagram, then the other half. Trim off excess paper on one sheet, overlap the papers so the parts of the diagram match, and tape them together.

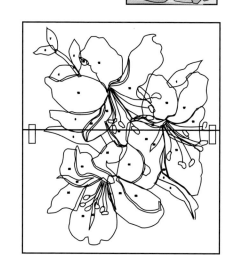

6. *Place the Bear Thread Pressing Sheet over the large diagram.*

If it is a little smaller than the diagram, that's okay. Try to have it cover at least part of each petal and leaf.

Tape the sheet in a couple of places to keep it from shifting. Avoid having the tape over any of the design lines.

7. *Arrange the pieces of fabric.*

Peel the paper backing off the pieces and place them on the pressing sheet, following the diagram.

Start with the back pieces (the **lower numbers)**. You can just finger press the pieces in place, then reposition them easily if you need to. Some pieces will overlap a little, and some might go beyond the edge of the pressing sheet.

If there has been some distortion in the design while enlarging it, pieces might be spread apart a little more or be closer together than in the drawing. Don't worry about it. This diagram is just to help you. You don't need to follow it slavishly. If you want to have a petal come in front of another instead of going in back (and it looks natural), that's okay.

Feeling creative?

*Instead of using a placement diagram, you can arrange the pieces freehand. Move pieces around as needed until everything fits. Remember that this is **your** design and you can make creative changes. You can even leave out a petal or leaf or add another one, if you wish.*

---

8. Choose the background fabric.

If you haven't chosen your background fabric, you can take the arrangement (still on the pressing sheet) and place it over several different fabrics to see which is best.

When you find the right background fabric, press it and cut it to the size you want.

9. Transfer the design to the background fabric.

Remove the design from the appliqué sheet. Just lift the design off, or turn everything over and peel the sheet off.

Place the design on the background fabric. Press it to hold it in place.

Now you are ready to finish the edges with Hot Ribbon. Directions begin on page 9.

Examples of embellishment with Hot Ribbon

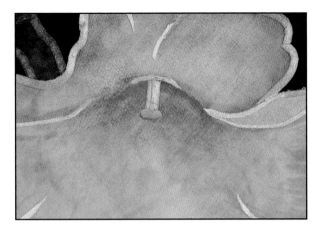

Angel Trumpet
Ribbon outlining the petals has been shaded with markers to create subtle blends. The details on the petals are added with split and tapered ribbon. See page 9 for tips on making the center.

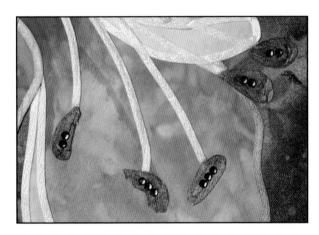

Enchanting Lilies
I'm an artist, not a botanist. I can't tell a stamen from a stovepipe, but I love using ribbon to create those things bees love in the center of the flower. (I also added Swarovski Crystals. See pages 68-69.)

Ribbon Colors

1. White
2. Red
3. Blue
4. Black
5. Purple
6. Blue Green
7. Lilac
8. Lemon
9. Maroon
10. Royal Blue
11. Lime Green
12. Sky Blue
13. Orange
14. Forest green
15. Dark blue
16. Fuchsia
17. Honey
18. Gray
19. Golden yellow
20. Dark brown
21 Metallic Gold
22 Metallic Silver

Exotic Hibiscus
Here's my way of applying ribbon. I'm left-handed; you might use the opposite hands.

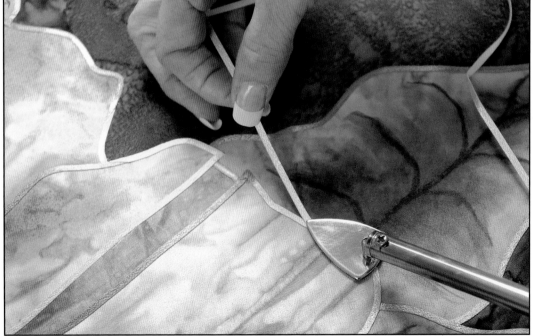

How to use Hot Ribbon

Hot Ribbon is a 1/8" wide fusible ribbon from Japan. It's great for finishing the edges of the appliqué and creating graceful curving lines. Just iron it on with a mini-iron!

1. Choose the best color of ribbon.

I list with each project the colors I used, but you might choose different ones to match your fabric. I often use a somewhat lighter color, then shade the ribbon with permanent markers, subtly blending colors, before or after applying it to the fabric.

2. Preheat the Clover Mini-Iron on a medium setting for a few minutes.

The metal part is very hot, so park it in a large mug for safety.
While it's heating, arrange a padded working surface and spread out your project.

3. Apply the ribbon.

Making sure the adhesive side is down, the shiny side up, attach the ribbon to a starting point, covering the edge of the fabric. Bond a few seconds.

Guide the ribbon (don't pull it) as you guide the iron with the other hand.

Hold the iron any way that's comfortable for you.

You'll want to practice on scraps first. A good way is to find a large floral print and practice outlining the leaves and petals.

Ribbon will melt and go around gentle curves, but when you come to a sharp angle, cut the ribbon carefully with sharp scissors and use a new piece.

Avoid building up too many layers of ribbon.

You sometimes need to create details like this flower center (top photo).

If you make a mistake or change your mind, reheat the ribbon and pull it off. Replace it with a new piece.

Clip corners to round them.

4. Bond permanently.

Using a pressing sheet, press for 35-40 seconds with a regular iron (medium hot).

The project is washable, but, as with any fine quilt, you should avoid washing it too much. And avoid hot dryers or other heat sources which might make the ribbon come loose.

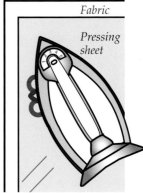

Fabric

Pressing sheet

Supplies

Fabric:

Use 100% cotton, as you would for any fine quilt.

Fabric for the flowers
Use subtle batiks or other variegated fabrics, no prints or hard stripes. The amount of fabric listed for a project allows for "fussy cutting" (arranging pattern pieces to take advantage of differences in hues or shades of light and dark).

Fabric for the borders and backing
Now you can look for prints to complement the design. Don't use prints that are brighter and bolder than the design. They would be an unpleasant distraction.

Batting
Get lightweight batting slightly larger than the project after borders are applied. I prefer Soft & Bright cotton batting by Warm Co..

Other supplies and tools:

Most of the supplies I use are shown on the opposite page, arranged from left to right.

- **Hot Ribbon.** See page 8.
- **Markers** (optional) to modify ribbon colors and shade petals and leaves. I usually use Copic markers, which come in hundreds of colors and are refillable.
- **Rotary cutter, ruler, and mat.**
- **Sharpie marker** (optional) good for tracing the pattern pieces.
- **Straight pins and seam ripper.** These (plus a **sewing machine, thread, and other standard sewing supplies**) are used for borders and binding.
- **Two pairs of scissors**, a large pair and a small sharp pair for precisely trimming ribbon.
- **Steam-a-Seam2 fusible web.** Projects take anywhere from two to five 9" x 12" sheets.
- **A Bear Thread Applique Pressing Sheet.** You'll find the 18" x 20" size most useful.
- **Fray-check** (optional) to finish raw edges if Hot Ribbon isn't used.
- **A regular iron** and perhaps a travel iron for small areas.
- **A Clover Mini Iron.** Clover's carrying case is also handy so you can put the iron away while it's hot.
- **A large mug.** Use it to park your hot iron, saving table space and avoiding accidents.
- **Steel wool.** I keep some handy in a little tin to clean the mini-iron.

Not shown
- **A padded surface** - A large June Taylor pressing board is nice, but folded towels will do.
- **Swarovski Crystals** and the tool to apply them with. These are optional. See pages 68-69.

Good fabrics:

Coordinated with Ribbon
Since Hot Ribbon colors are limited, you might get it first, then choose fabrics to match.

Subtle stripes
Place pattern pieces carefully so these streaks make the leaves and petals look realistic.

Shades of light and dark
Get depth in petals and leaves by taking advantage of the darker areas.

Multi-colored
One fabric might substitute for two or three on the list.

Supplies:
These are described on page 10.

11

Timeless Tulips

Project size with borders is about 19" x 24". Directions start on page 13.

Timeless Tulips

With my Dutch heritage, it is only natural for me to have tulips for my first project. Tulips are timeless, having been cultivated for at least 3,000 years. The tulip industry is giving us new colors and shapes all the time, but the old fashioned tulips remain my favorites. I've kept this first project simple so everyone will feel comfortable attempting it. I used a dark background to give more contrast and a dramatic look but feel free to experiment.

Project size with borders is about 19" x 24". The inner border is 1" wide and the outer border is 3".

Supplies

You will need the general supplies and tools listed on page 10, plus these supplies.

Fabric:
Fat quarter for background
1/8 yard, or scraps of each of these fabrics:
    Dark green
    Light green
    Purple
    Yellow
1/8 yard of one tulip color for the inner border
3/4 yard print fabric for outer border and binding
3/4 yard print fabric for backing
Batting about 26" x 33"

Steam-a-Seam2:
2 sheets

Hot Ribbon:
1 Lemon Yellow #8
1 Purple #5
1 Lilac #7
1 Lime Green #11
1 Forest Green #14

Making Timeless Tulips

Here's how the steps on pages 5-9 apply to Timeless Tulips.

- **Trace the pieces on Steam-a-Seam2.**

- **Cut pieces out and press them to the back of the fabrics.**
  Any streaks of color should go this way on the petals.

- **Cut out the pieces carefully.**

- **Enlarge the placement guide 120%.**

- **Place the applique sheet over the placement guide.**

- **Arrange the pieces.**
  Do all the leaf and stem pieces first, starting with the lower numbers, then the petals.

- **Cut background fabric about 14" x 19".**

- **Transfer the arrangement to the background fabric.**

  Tip: Does the dark background show through the yellow fabric? Make a shield. Press Steam-a-Seam2 to a 4" square of of muslin. Bond the yellow pieces (A-1, A-2, and A-3) to it. Trim the shapes and apply as usual.

- **Apply Hot Ribbon.**
  See pages 8 and 9.

- **Do final bonding with a large iron.**

- **Add borders.**
  Directions are on pages 72 and 73.

- **Quilt the project.**
  See page 74.

- **Add a hanging sleeve, bind the edges, and add a label.**
  See page 75.

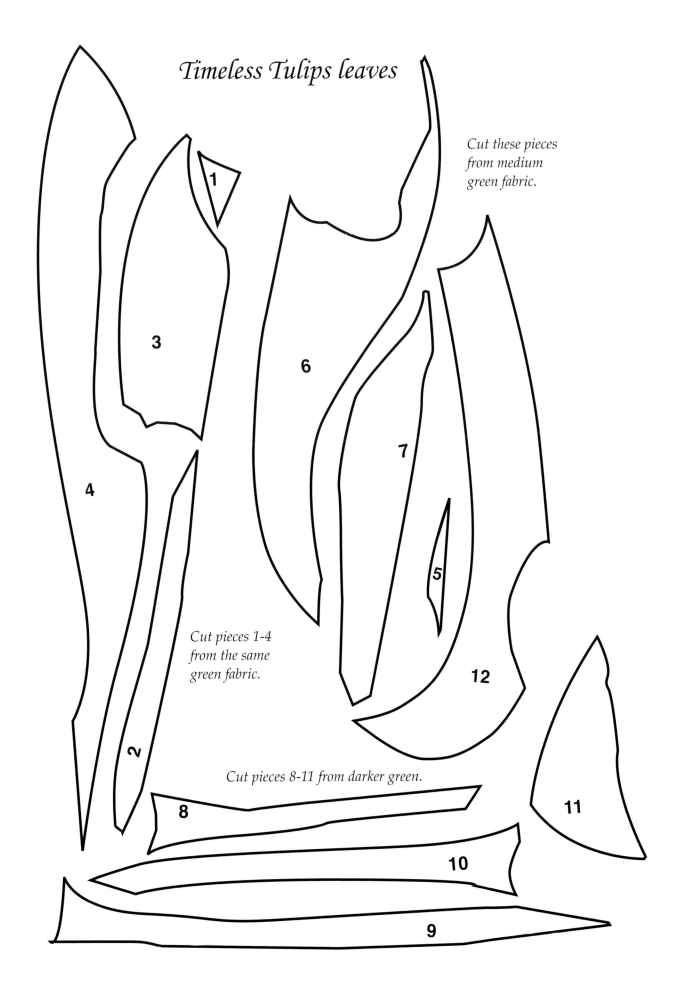

Timeless Tulips leaves

Cut these pieces from medium green fabric.

1

3

6

7

4

5

12

Cut pieces 1-4 from the same green fabric.

2

Cut pieces 8-11 from darker green.

8

11

10

9

Tulip petals

Since the tulip is a simple design, you can easily compare the shapes with the colored photo and decide the fabric for each piece. (You can change your tulips to other colors, of course.)

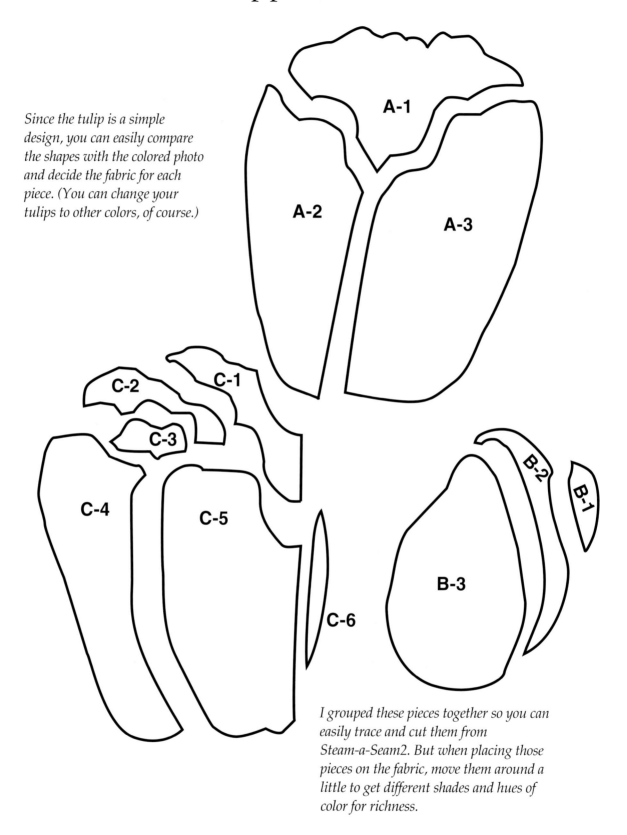

A-1

A-2

A-3

C-2

C-1

C-3

C-4

C-5

C-6

B-2

B-1

B-3

I grouped these pieces together so you can easily trace and cut them from Steam-a-Seam2. But when placing those pieces on the fabric, move them around a little to get different shades and hues of color for richness.

Tulips placement guide

Enlarge this diagram 120%
(to legal size).

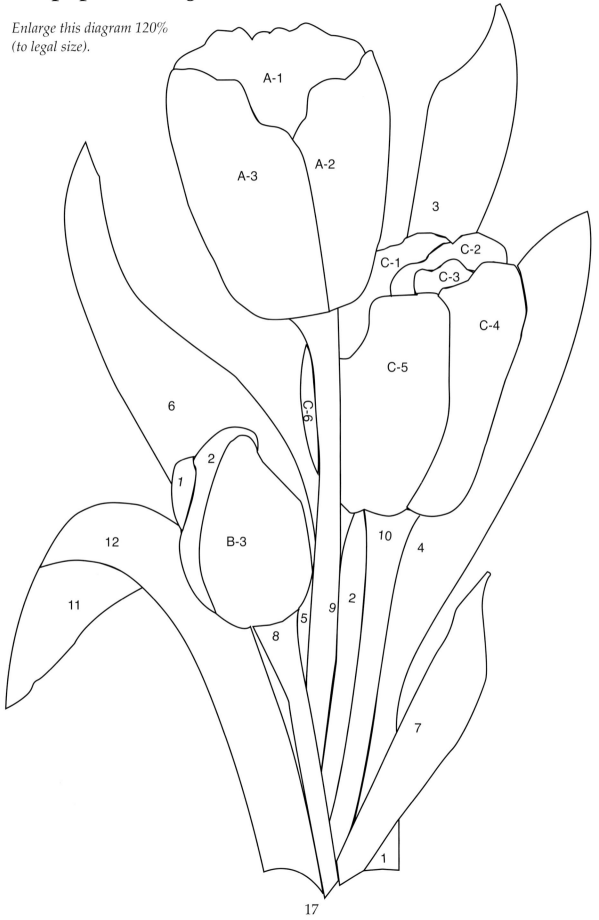

Enchanting Lilies

Many years ago one of my students brought in a picture of lilies for an art project. I was so drawn to the picture that the student gave it to me after he no longer needed it. I've kept the picture all these years and found it once again as I was looking for various flower types to use for quilt patterns. Lilies have an enchanting quality that makes me think of magical moments in fairy tales. I hope you too will get caught up in their magic as you create the whole flower from the many pieces.

Shown in color on page 25.

Project size with borders is about 29-1/2" x 35". It has a 1-1/2" inner border and a 3" outer border.

Supplies

You will need the general supplies and tools listed on page 10, plus these supplies.

Fabric:
3/4 yard for background
1/4 yard of variegated pink
1/8 yard of lighter pink
1/8 yard of variegated green (or scraps)
1/4 yard for the inner border
3/4 yard print fabric for outer border and binding
1 yard print fabric for backing
Batting about 42" x 39"

Crystals (optional)
50 of #33 Smoked Topaz

Steam-a-Seam2:
4 sheets

Hot Ribbon:
1 Lime Green #11
1 Forest Green #14
1 Gray #18
1 Dark Brown # 20
3 White #1
3 Pink #16

Making Enchanting Lilies

Create the design.

See pages 5-7. This design has a lot of pieces, so have several bags or envelopes to store them in. The leaves and stems (below) will be placed first, then the A, B, and C pieces, starting with the low numbers. The pink highlights are placed last.

Embellish the design with Hot Ribbon and crystals.

The lilies have graceful filaments coming out from the center of each flower. Just draw wobbly lines freehand with light colored ribbon. See a closeup on page 8. For the crystals, see page 39 and pages 68-69.

Add borders (pages 72-73).

To match the sample, cut the inner borders 2" wide, outer borders 4".

Finish the quilt.

Quilt and bind the project with your favorite methods, or see pages 74-75.

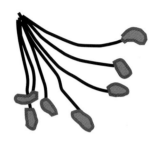

Enchanting Lilies leaves and stems

Cut these pieces from various shades of green.

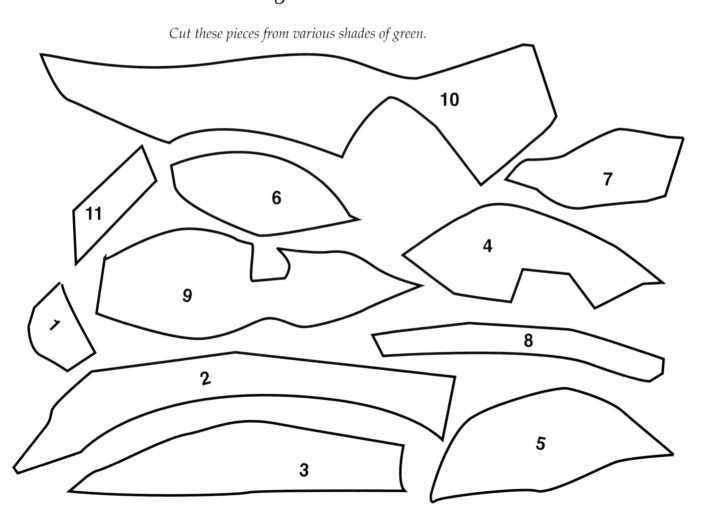

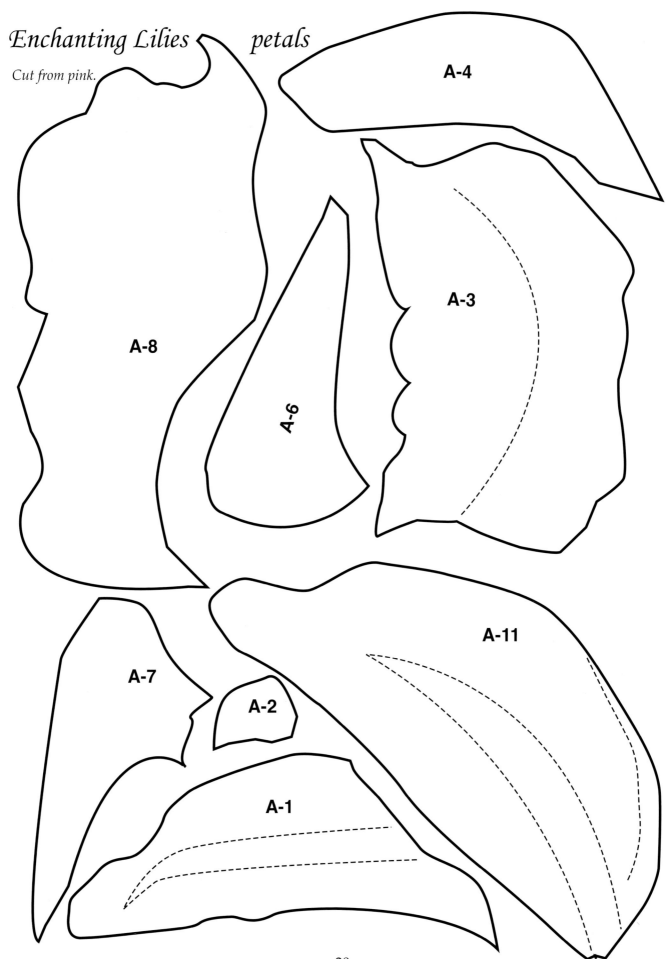

Enchanting Lilies   petals

Cut from pink.

A-4

A-3

A-8

A-6

A-11

A-7

A-2

A-1

20

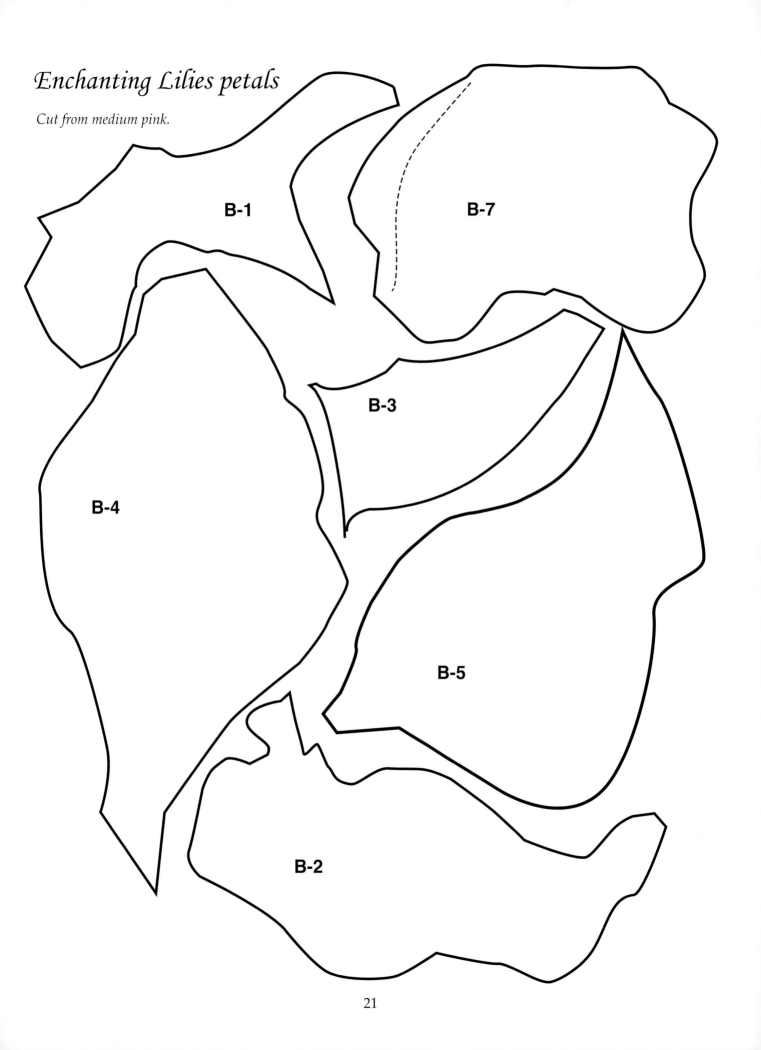

Enchanting Lilies petals

Cut from medium pink.

B-1

B-7

B-3

B-4

B-5

B-2

21

Enchanting Lilies petals

Cut from dark and medium pink.

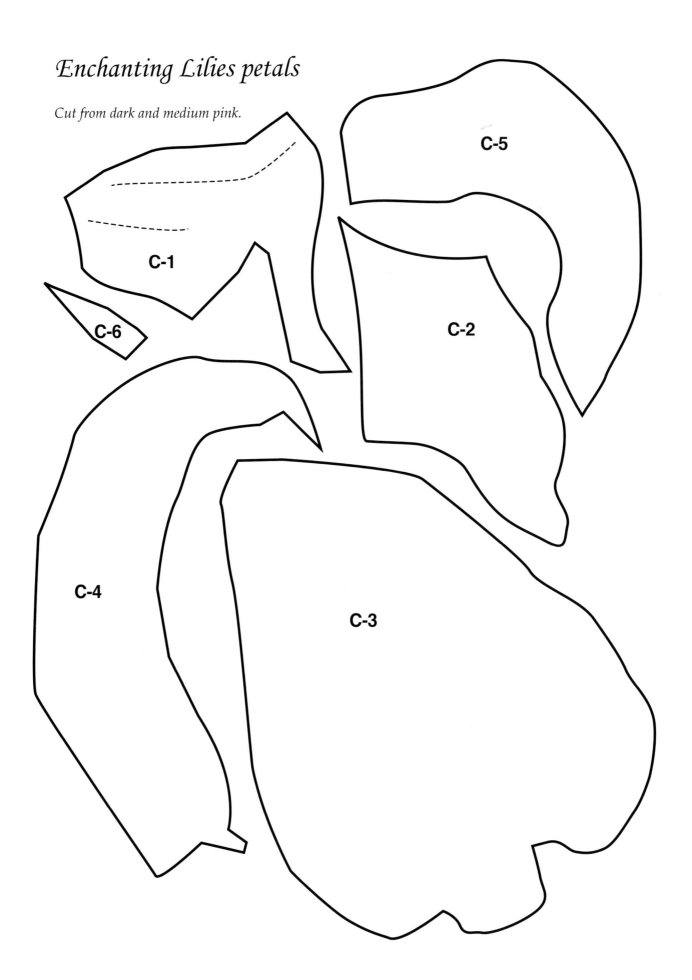

C-5

C-1

C-6

C-2

C-4

C-3

Enchanting Lilies highlights

These should be cut from light pink.

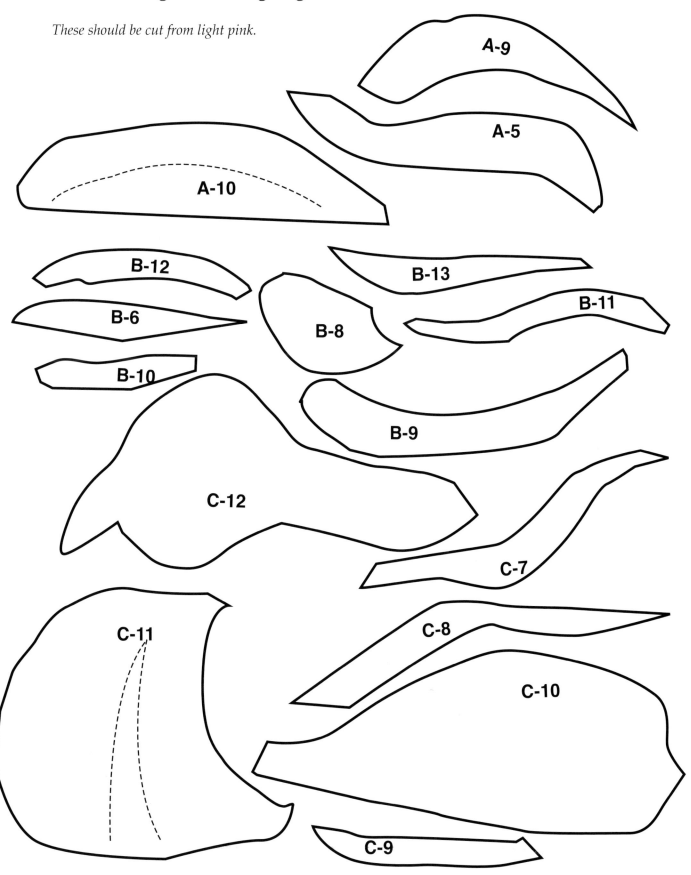

Enchanting Lilies placement guide

Enlarge this diagram 200%.

Enchanting Lilies

Project size with borders is about 29-1/2" x 35". Directions begin on page 19.

Angel Trumpet

Project size with borders is about 28" x 34". Directions begin on page 27.

Angel Trumpets

A friend of mine introduced me recently to Angel Trumpets and I fell in love with their graceful shape and sweet aroma. I can almost hear the angels blowing their trumpets. The plant is large enough that the clusters of long slender flowers hang down at face level as if to ensure that we do not miss any of beauty and perfume. The pattern has a cluster of 5 flowers but can be made with fewer or more flowers to give it the look you want.

Project size is about 28" x 34 "with a 1" inner border and a 3" outer border.

Supplies

You will need the general supplies and tools listed on page 10, plus these supplies.

Fabric:
5/8 yard for background
1/4 yard variegated pink
1/8 yard or scraps of green
1/4 yard for the inner border
3/4 yard print fabric for outer border and binding
1 yard print fabric for backing
Batting about 32" x 38"

Steam-a-Seam2:
4 sheets

Hot Ribbon:
2 Forest Green #14
3 White #1 or Pink #16

Making Angel Trumpets

Create the design.
See pages 5-7.
• Notice how the ends of the flowers have a delicate shading. If you don't have fabric with shades of pink and yellow-green, plan to create this with markers.
• See page 28 for some notes about enlarging the placement diagram.

Embellish it with Hot Ribbon.
See pages 8 and 9. Notice the close-up photo and tips for making the center of the top flower.

Finish the quilt.
Add borders (pages 72-73). Quilt and bind it with your favorite methods, or see pages 74-75.

Angel Trumpet leaves

Cut from green.

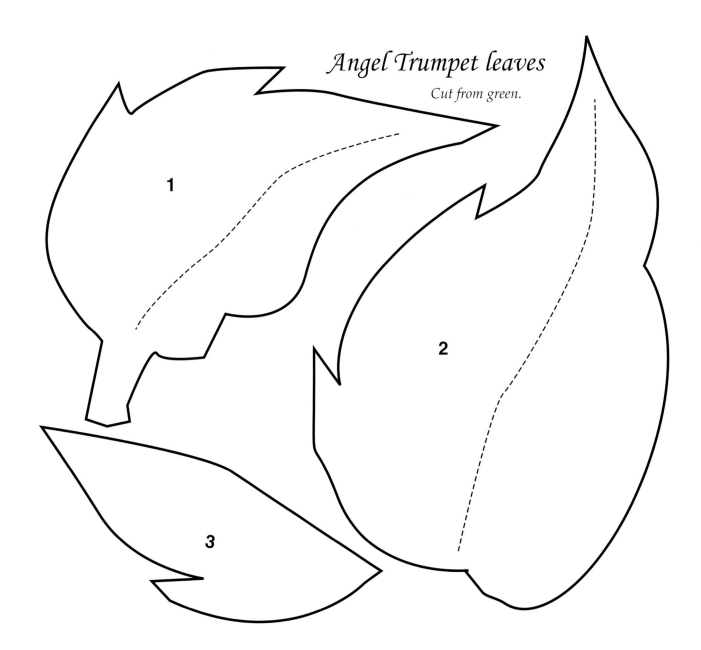

1

2

3

Three ways to enlarge the placement diagram.

Enlarged on one 11 x 17 sheet; some will be cut off, but it will still work.

Enlarged on two 11 x 17 sheets, taped together overlapping a bit.

Enlarged on three legal size sheets, taped together, overlapping a bit.

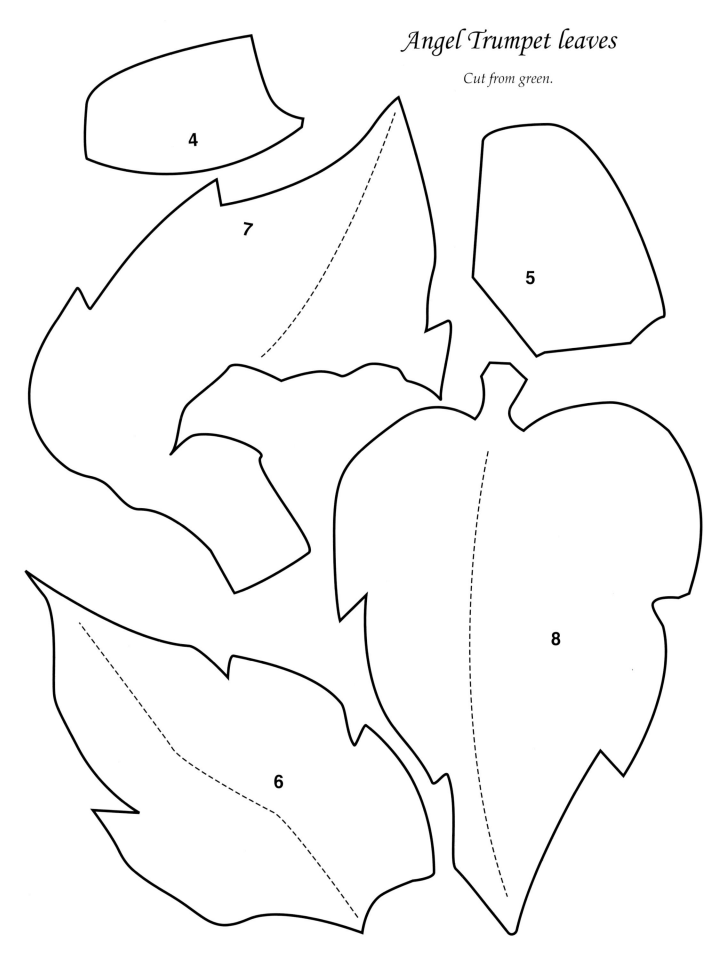

Angel Trumpet leaves

Cut from green.

4

7

5

8

6

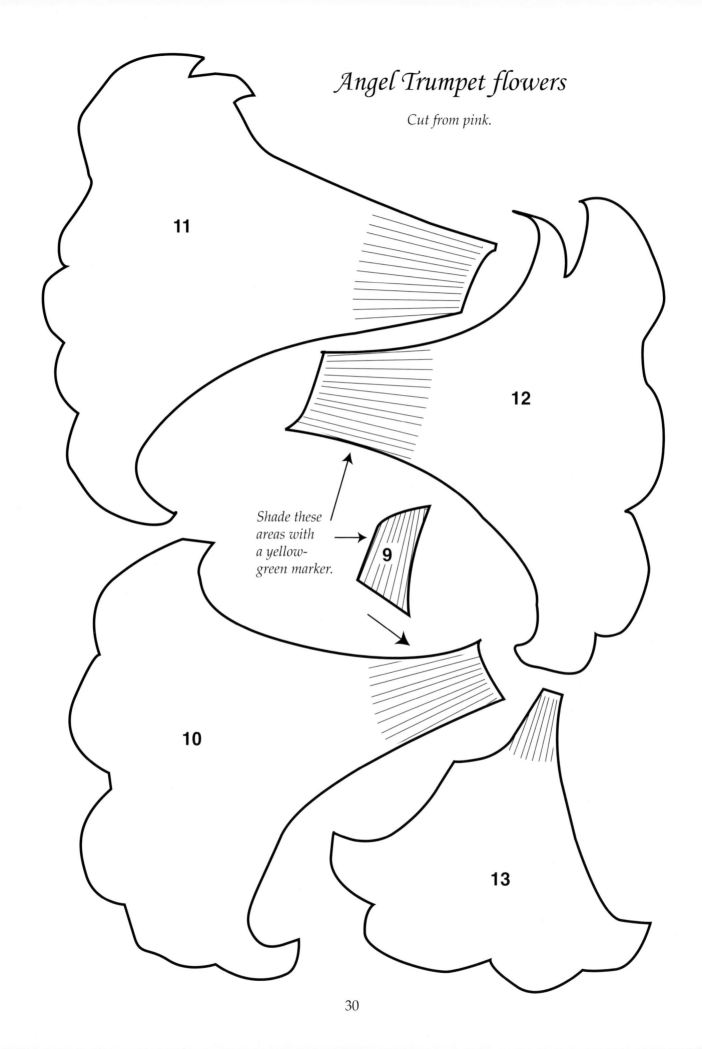

Angel Trumpet flowers

Cut from pink.

11

12

Shade these
areas with
a yellow-
green marker.

9

10

13

30

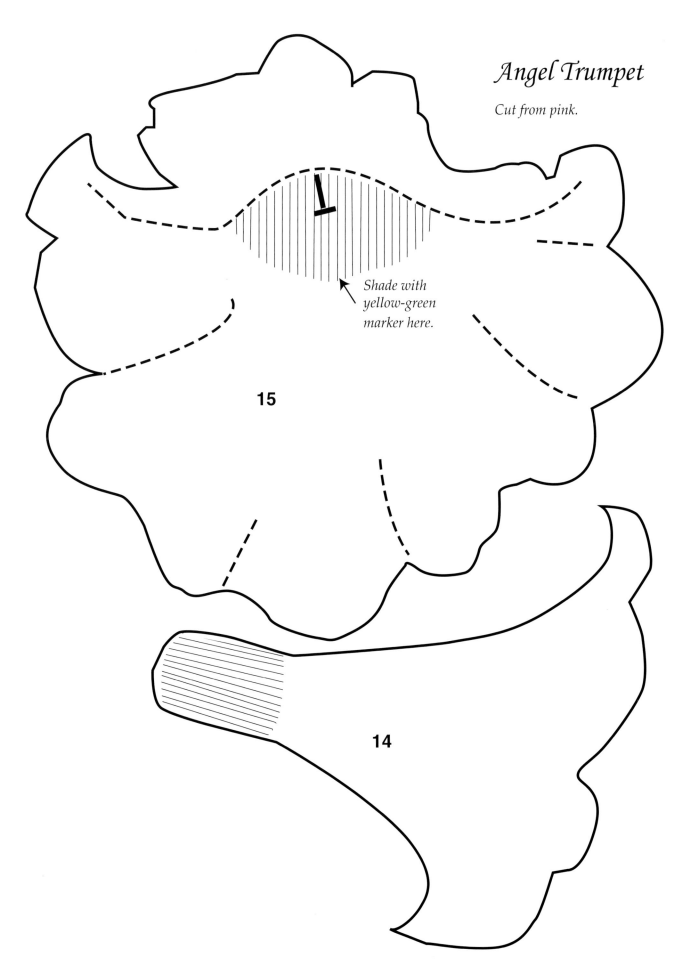

Angel Trumpet

Cut from pink.

Shade with
yellow-green
marker here.

15

14

31

Angel Trumpet Placement Guide

Enlarge 200%.
(Edges will be cut off; that's okay.)

Romantic Peony

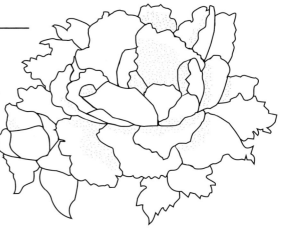

When I see a peony, I think of romance and elegance, of the Victorian age with stately homes and beautiful gardens. Peonies have been around a long time and never have lost their appeal. I have seen them in vivid colors, but I wanted a soft effect, so I chose pink. I was very pleased with the result, and it became my favorite pattern in this book. Make your own romantic statement with this peony.

Shown in color on page 39 and 40.

Project size with borders is about 34" x 29". This project has a narrow pink border, a narrow green border, and a 4" outer border.

Supplies
You will need the general supplies and tools listed on page 10, plus these supplies.

Fabric:
  5/8 yard for background
  1/4 yard variegated pink
  1/8 yard or scraps of:
    Dark green
    Light green
    Pale pink
  A scrap of yellow for the center
  1/8 yard of pink for the narrow border
  1/4 yard green for the 1" border
  3/4 yard print fabric for outer border and binding
  1 yard print fabric for backing
  Batting about 37" x 31"

Steam-a-Seam2:
  4 sheets

Hot Ribbon:
  1 Lime Green #11
  1 Forest Green #14
  1 Golden Yellow #19
  2 White #1
  2 Pink #16

Crystals (optional)
  25 of #11

Making Romantic Peony

Create the design.
See pages 5-7. Shading is important in this design. Copy the shading on the pattern pieces and use the darker areas of fabric (or shade with markers). Study page 39 to see how to do the center.

Embellish the design with Hot Ribbon and crystals.
See pages 8-9, page 39, and pages 68-69.

Finish the quilt.
Add borders (pages 72-73). Quilt and bind it with your favorite methods, or see pages 74-75.

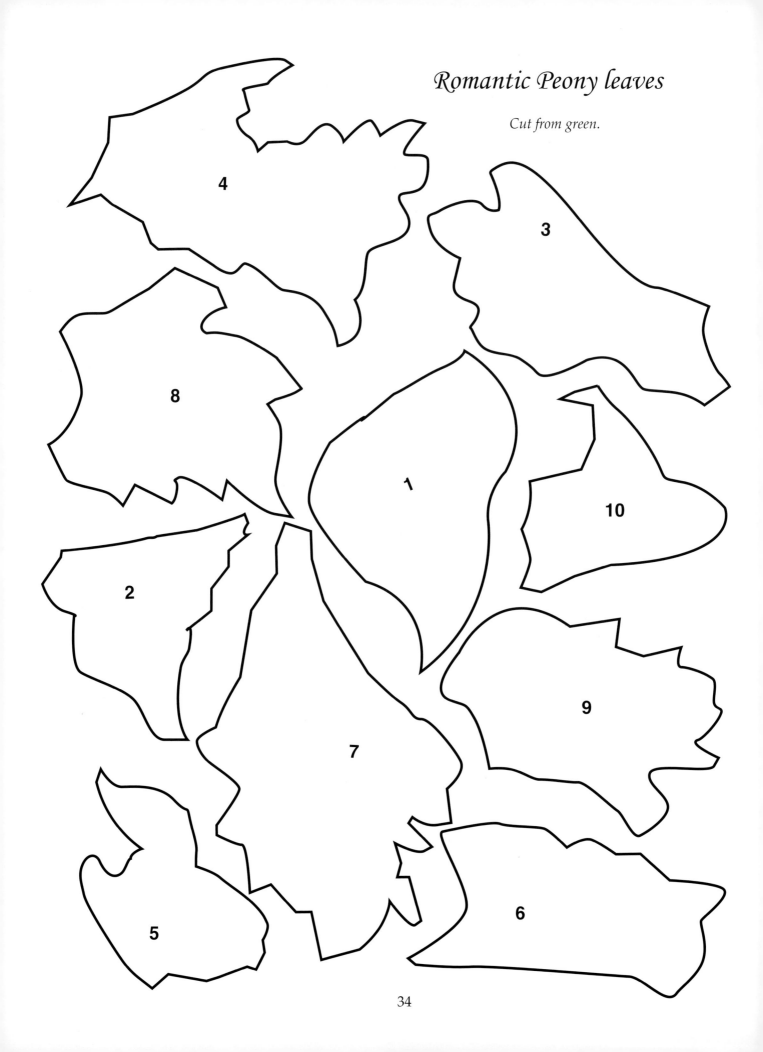

Romantic Peony leaves

Cut from green.

Romantic Peony petals

Cut from pink. Pay attention to the shading.

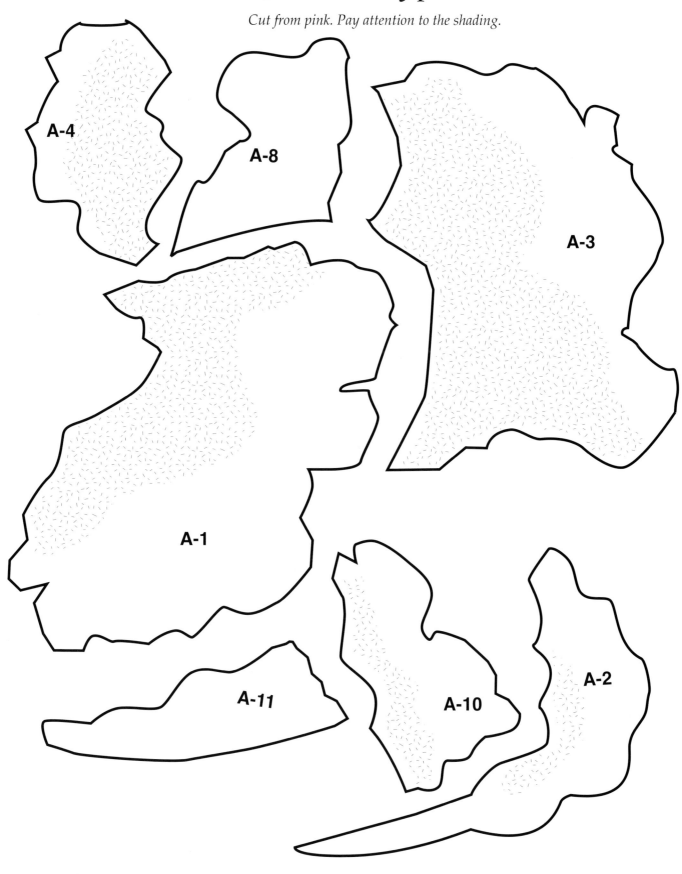

Romantic Peony petals

Cut from pink. Pay attention to the shading.

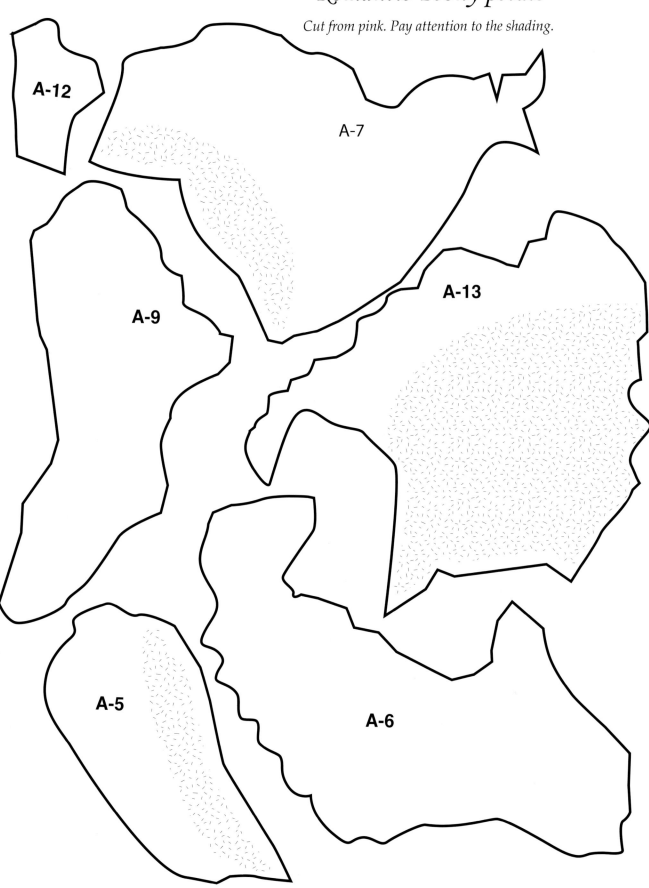

Romantic Peony petals
Cut from pink.

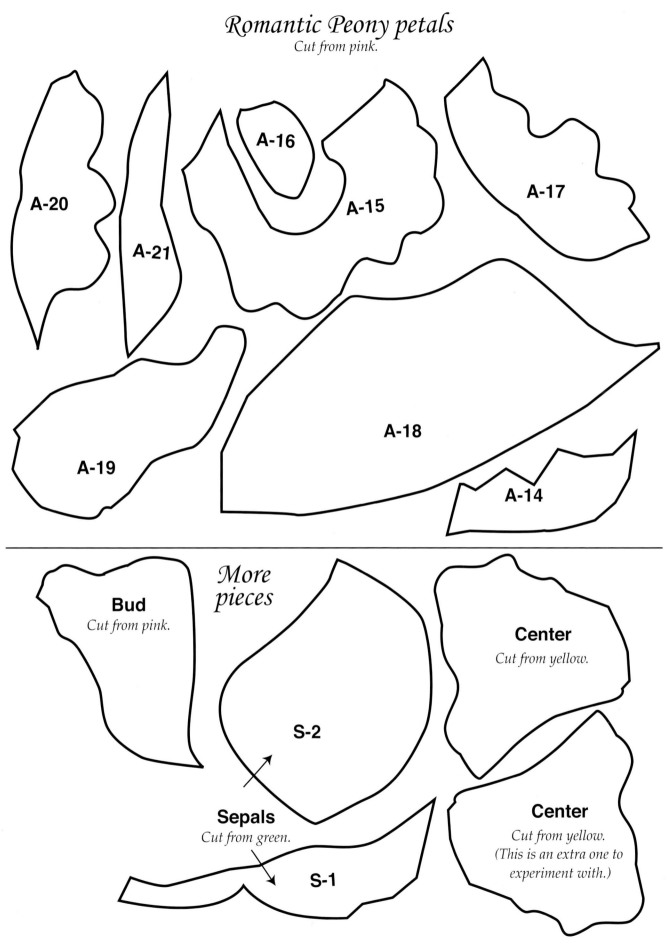

A-20

A-21

A-16

A-15

A-17

A-19

A-18

A-14

More pieces

Bud
Cut from pink.

S-2

Center
Cut from yellow.

Sepals
Cut from green.

S-1

Center
Cut from yellow.
(This is an extra one to experiment with.)

Romantic Peony placement guide

Enlarge 200%.
(Copy one half, then the other, and tape them together.)

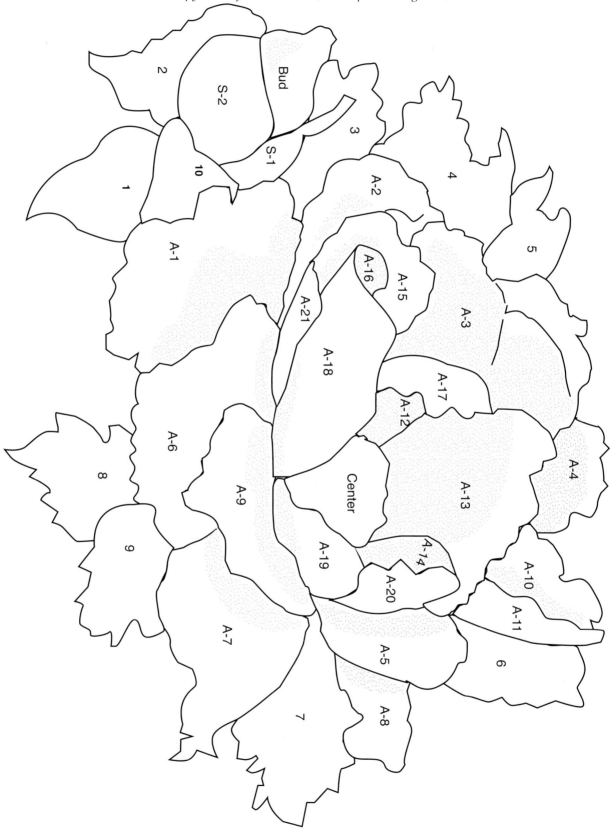

The center of the Peony

I fussed with the center of the flower until I got it right. I was pleased at how realistic it looked, and other people gushed about it. Here's a close-up view.

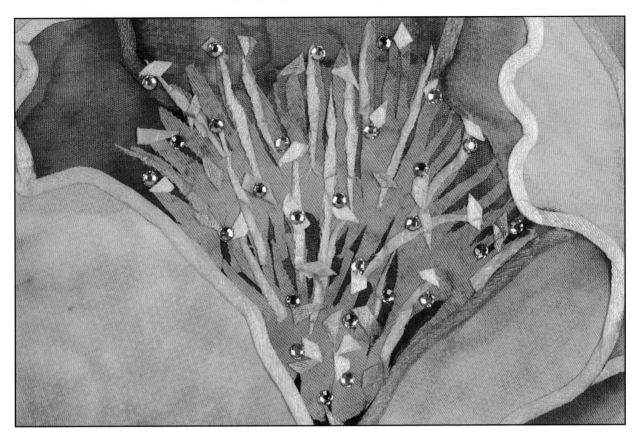

How to get this effect:

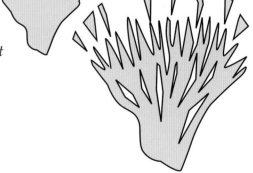

- Cut random triangles from the edges of one of the center pieces with small, sharp scissors. (You don't need to make yours match this one. If you goof, try again with the spare piece.) Save some of the little triangles.

- Bond the center piece to the design.

- Bond some of the little pieces onto the design, at different angles.

- Cut pointed pieces of the yellow Hot Ribbon and attach them in a random way.

- If you don't like the effect, reheat the pieces and pull them off. Apply other pieces.

- If you like the effect, add some Swarovsky Crystals, if you wish. See pages 68-69.

Project size with borders is about 34 " x 29". Directions begin on page 33.

Radiant Fuchsias

Project size with borders is about 35" x 36". Notice the close-up views on page 42.

Tips for making your Fuchsias radiant

Take time to find the right fabrics. Look for fabrics with subtle shades and hues, then cut each piece carefully to take advantage of the variations.

I often trace the pattern with a marker on a piece of Mylar, then place it over the fabric to isolate just the right spot.

It's also easy to trace the piece on paper, cut out a mask, and place it over the fabric.

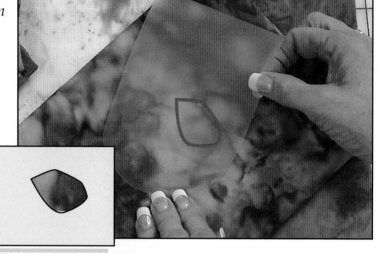

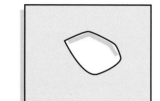

If the fabric doesn't have the exact coloration I need, I use permanent markers to add some subtle color, usually after the piece has been bonded onto the background. I enhanced the buds by shading them with a green marker.

These shapes are built up of two pieces of ribbon circled by a third piece. The outer edges were colored lightly with a purple marker so they looked fuzzy against the dark purple background. Crystals are added for the extra sparkle.

Radiant Fuchsias

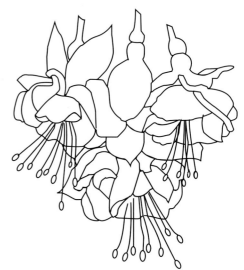

My earliest memories of fuchsias was seeing them in my grandparents' flower garden. They reminded me of ballerinas with dainty accessories. I was particularly attracted to them because I was taking ballet lessons at the time. I appreciate fuchsias even more now, as I see the intensity of their colors and how the clusters radiate a message of "Come look at me!" Your friends and family will also hear the call to look at your finished fuchsia quilt!

Project size with borders is about 35" x 36". The inner border is 1-1/2 and the outer border 3". Read the "Making Radiant Fuchsias" notes on pages 48-49 before starting.

Supplies

You will need the general supplies and tools listed on page 10, plus these supplies.

Fabric:
- 3/4 yard for background
- 1/3 yard total of 6 different pinks and purples
- Scraps of these fabrics:
    - Dark green
    - Light green
- 1/4 yard green for the inner border
- 3/4 yard print fabric for outer border and binding
- 1-1/8 yard print fabric for backing
- Batting about 40" square

Crystals (optional)
- 60 of #23 Light Rose

Steam-a-Seam2:
- 5 sheets

Hot Ribbon:
- 1 White #1
- 1 Red #2
- 1 Purple #5
- 1 Lime Green #11
- 1 Orange #13
- 1 Forest Green #14
- 2 Gray #18
- 4 Pink #16

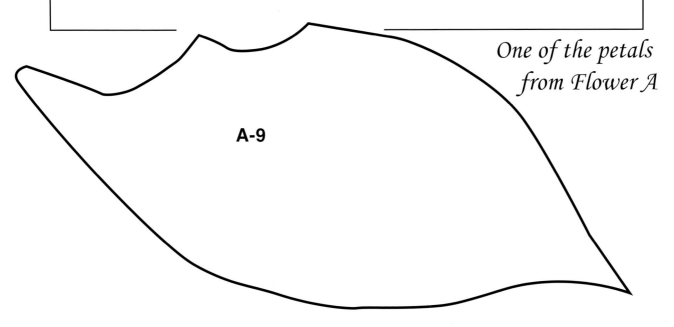

A-9

One of the petals from Flower A

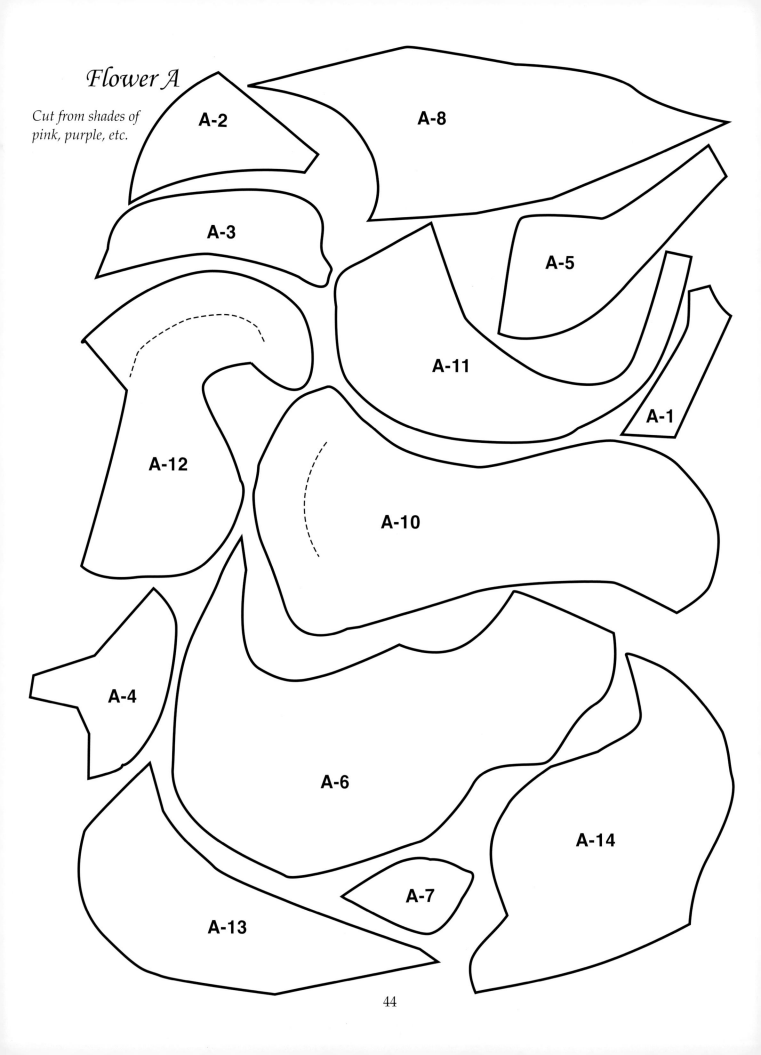

Flower A

Cut from shades of pink, purple, etc.

A-2

A-8

A-3

A-5

A-11

A-12

A-1

A-10

A-4

A-6

A-14

A-7

A-13

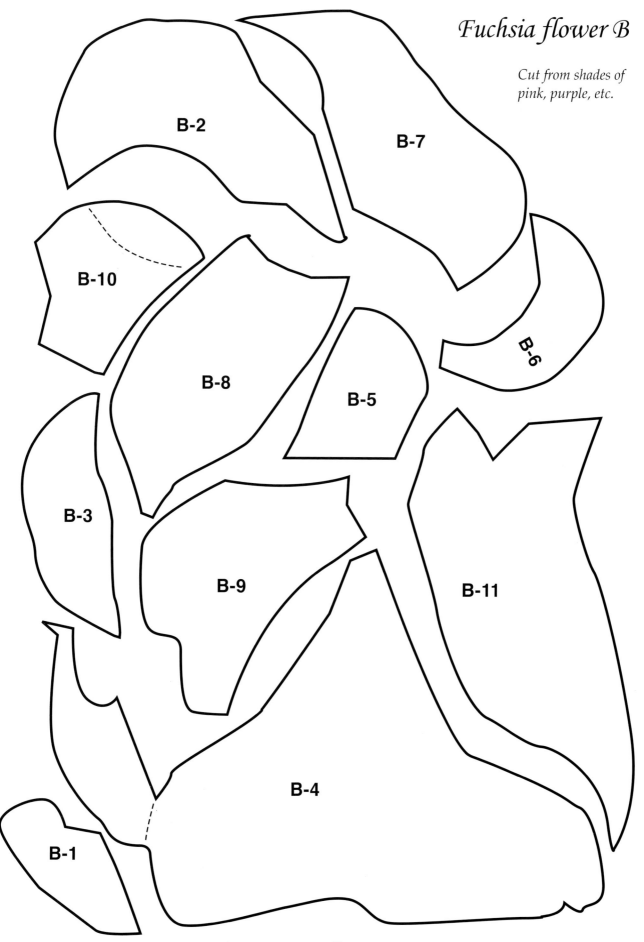

Fuchsia flower B

Cut from shades of pink, purple, etc.

B-2

B-7

B-10

B-8

B-5

B-6

B-3

B-9

B-11

B-4

B-1

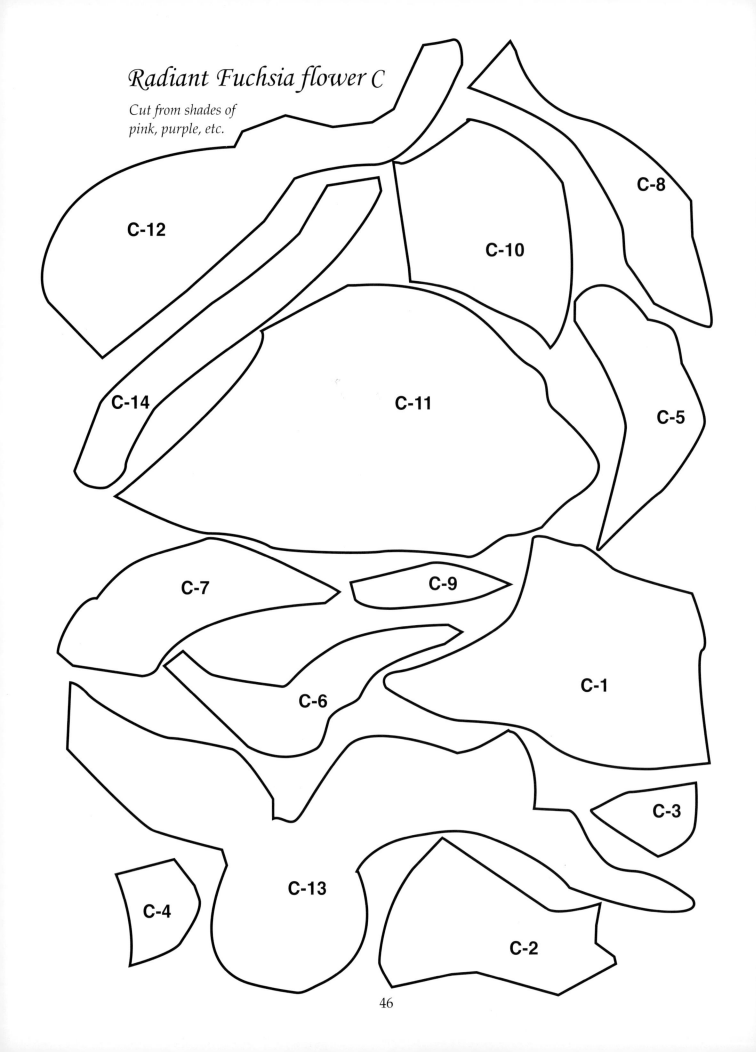

Radiant Fuchsia flower C

Cut from shades of
pink, purple, etc.

46

More Radiant Fuchsias pieces

Locate these leaves, buds, etc.
on the front cover photo
to see what fabrics to use.

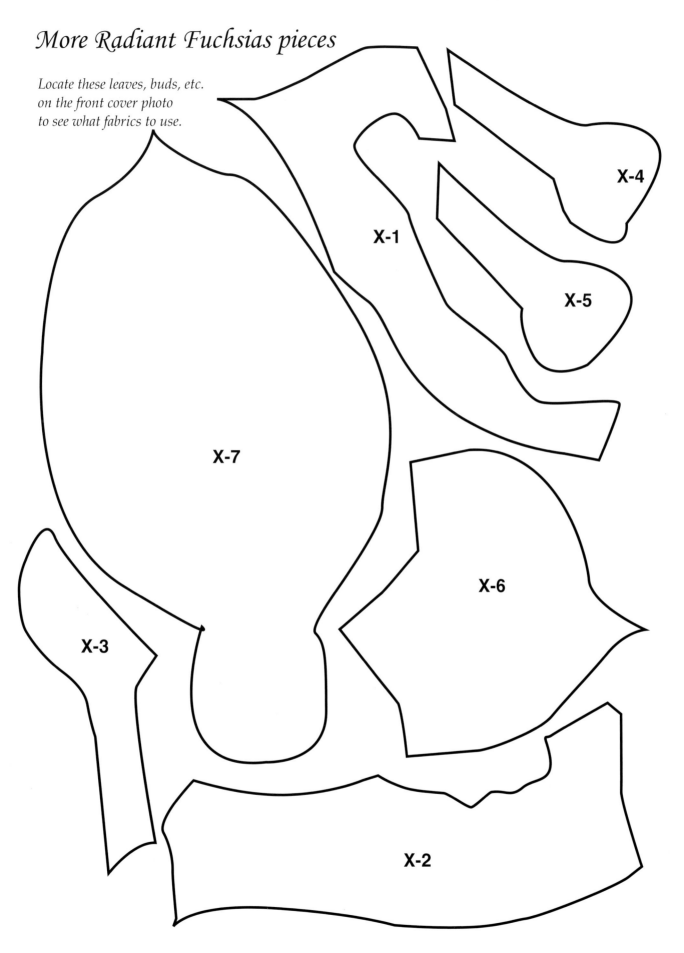

X-4

X-1

X-5

X-7

X-6

X-3

X-2

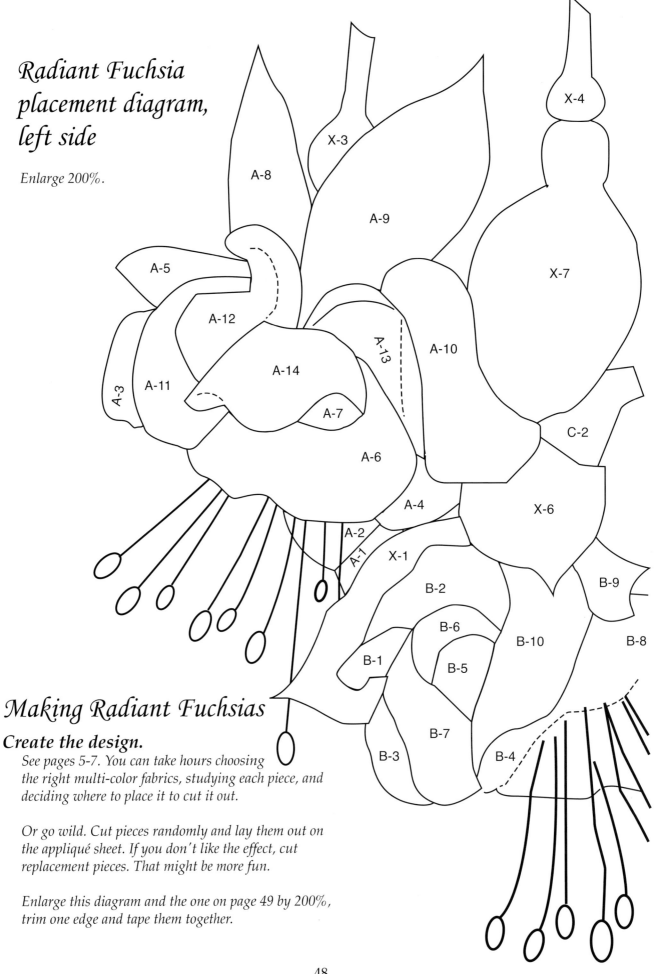

Radiant Fuchsia placement diagram, left side

Enlarge 200%.

A-8
X-3
A-9
X-4
A-5
X-7
A-12
A-13
A-10
A-14
A-7
A-3
A-11
C-2
A-6
A-4
X-6
A-2
A-1
X-1
B-9
B-2
B-6
B-10
B-8
B-1
B-5
B-7
B-3
B-4

Making Radiant Fuchsias

Create the design.

See pages 5-7. You can take hours choosing the right multi-color fabrics, studying each piece, and deciding where to place it to cut it out.

Or go wild. Cut pieces randomly and lay them out on the appliqué sheet. If you don't like the effect, cut replacement pieces. That might be more fun.

Enlarge this diagram and the one on page 49 by 200%, trim one edge and tape them together.

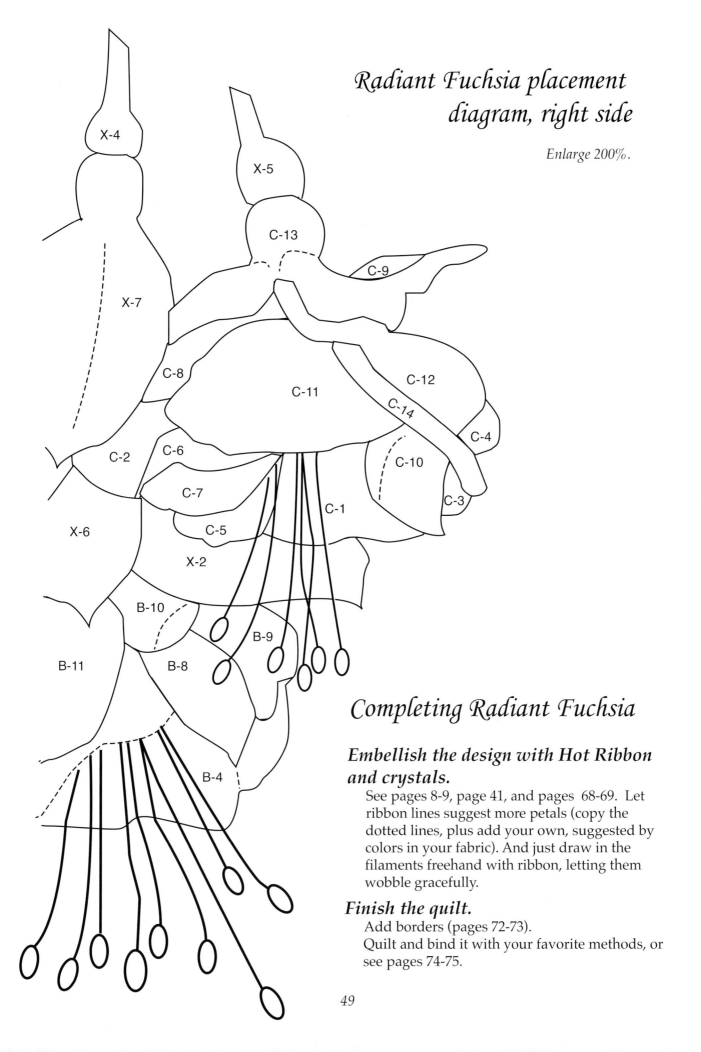

Radiant Fuchsia placement diagram, right side

Enlarge 200%.

Labels in diagram: X-4, X-5, C-13, C-9, X-7, C-8, C-12, C-11, C-14, C-4, C-2, C-6, C-10, C-3, C-7, C-1, X-6, C-5, X-2, B-10, B-9, B-11, B-8, B-4

Completing Radiant Fuchsia

Embellish the design with Hot Ribbon and crystals.

See pages 8-9, page 41, and pages 68-69. Let ribbon lines suggest more petals (copy the dotted lines, plus add your own, suggested by colors in your fabric). And just draw in the filaments freehand with ribbon, letting them wobble gracefully.

Finish the quilt.

Add borders (pages 72-73).
Quilt and bind it with your favorite methods, or see pages 74-75.

Exotic Orchids

Orchids conjure up visions of far-away tropical lands, probably because that's where we know they originated. Orchids used to be quite rare, found only in flower arrangements used for special occasions, like weddings and proms. I had them in my wedding bouquet, and ever since they have a special place in my heart. Orchids have continued to grow in popularity and many people have mastered the skills of growing them in their homes. However, I can not seem to get an orchid plant to bloom. My solution was to create a quilt pattern with orchids so I can enjoy their beauty without the challenge of growing them!

See this project in color on page 55

This project is about 35" x 28", including a 1" inner border and a 3" outer border.

Supplies

You will need the general supplies and tools listed on page 10, plus these supplies:

Fabric:
5/8 yard for background
1/4 yard yellow for the flowers
Scraps of:
    Dark brown for the stem
    Light brown for the stem
    Pink for flower centers
1/3 yard for the inner border
3/4 yard print fabric for outer border and binding
3/4 yard print fabric for backing
Batting about 39" x 32"

Steam-a-Seam2:
3 sheets

Hot Ribbon:
1 Maroon #9
1 Pink #16
1 Dark Brown #20
2 White #1
2 Lemon Yellow #8

Making Exotic Orchids

Create the design.
See pages 5-7.

Embellish the design with Hot Ribbon.
See pages 8-9

Finish the quilt.
Add borders (pages 72-73). Quilt and bind it with your favorite methods, or see pages 74-75.

Exotic Orchids, flowers A and B

Cut all these pieces from yellow.
Pay attention to the shading.

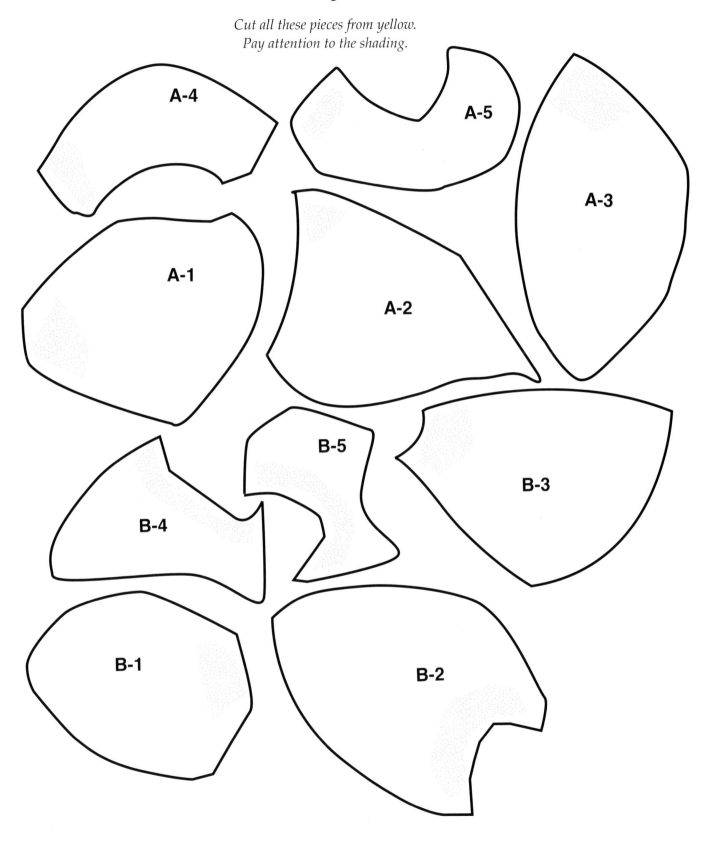

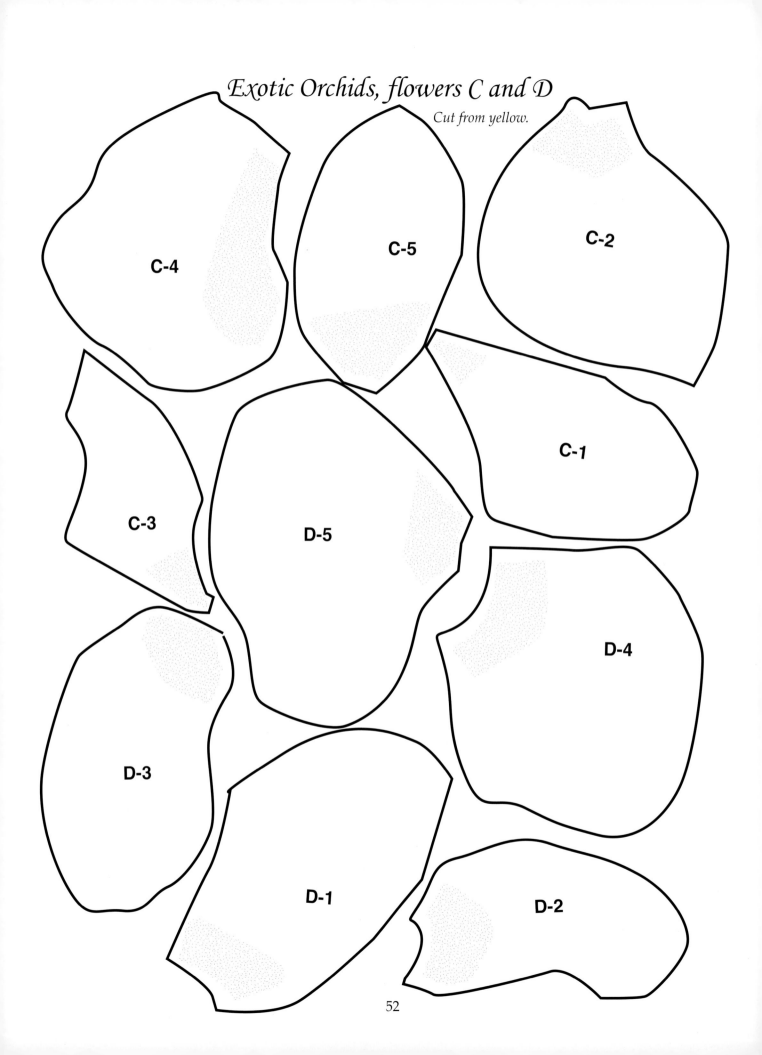

Exotic Orchids, flowers C and D

Cut from yellow.

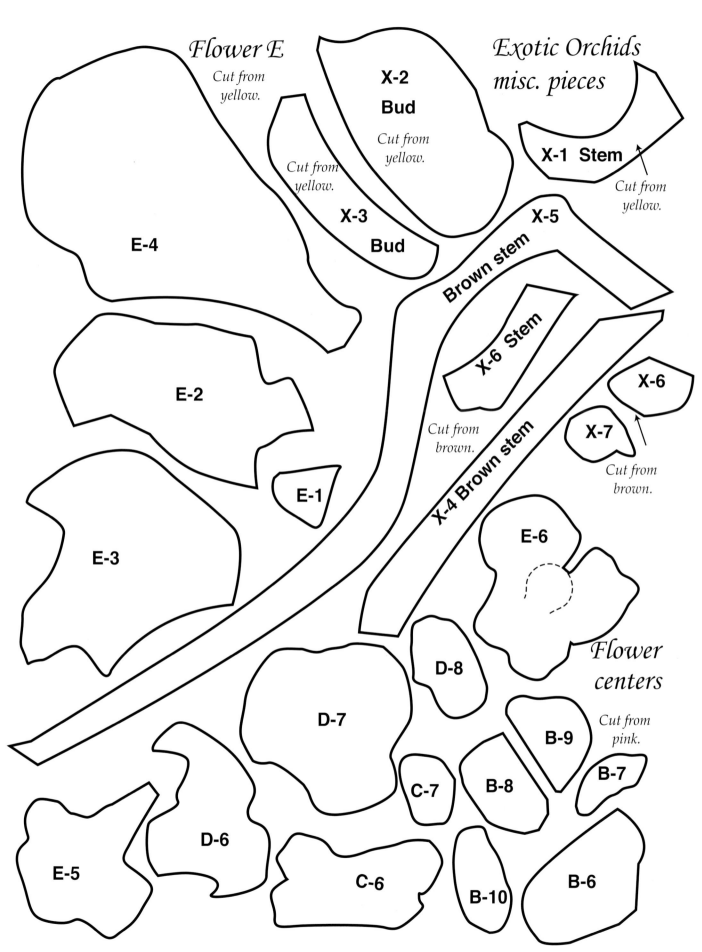

Flower E

Cut from yellow.

X-2 Bud

Cut from yellow.

Exotic Orchids misc. pieces

X-1 Stem

Cut from yellow.

Cut from yellow.

X-3 Bud

E-4

X-5

Brown stem

X-6 Stem

X-6

Cut from brown.

X-4 Brown stem

X-7

Cut from brown.

E-2

E-1

E-3

E-6

Flower centers

Cut from pink.

D-8

D-7

B-9

B-7

C-7

B-8

D-6

E-5

C-6

B-10

B-6

Exotic Orchids placement guide

Enlarge 200%.

Exotic Orchids

Project size with borders is about 35" x 28". Directions begin on page 50.

Trumpet Vine

Project size with borders is about 26" x 20". Directions begin on page 57.

Trumpet Vine

I was attracted to the trumpet vine because of its simplicity and aura of cheerfulness. Although the vine is considered a weed in some parts of the United States, I find the bright red trumpet-shaped flowers to be a nice addition to my flower collection. When I discovered that the trumpet vine attracts hummingbirds, I knew it was a "winner." You can have a winner too when you create your trumpet vine with flowers of deep red or your favorite shade of scarlet, orange, or peach.

Project size with borders is about 26" x 20". There is a 1" inner border and 3" outer border.

Supplies

You will need the general supplies and tools listed on page 10, plus these supplies.

Fabric:
1/2 yard for background
1/4 yard red for flowers
Scraps of green
1/4 yard for the inner border
3/4 yard print fabric for outer border and binding
1-1/8 yard print fabric for backing
Batting about 30" x 24"

Steam-a-Seam2:
3 sheets

Hot Ribbon:
2 Red #2
1 Lime Green #11
1 Orange #13
1 Forest Green #14

Making Trumpet Vine

This is one of the easiest projects, good for your first try!

Create the design.
Follow directions on pages 5-7.
Cut background fabric about 14" x 19".

Transfer the arrangement to the background fabric.

Apply Hot Ribbon.
See pages 8 and 9.

There are a lot of tendrils which you can just add freehand, curling and twisting around however you wish. Make just a few or as many as I did; it's your choice. Remember, if one doesn't look right, you just reheat it, pull it off and try again.

Do final bonding with a large iron.

Add borders.
Directions are on pages 72 and 73.

Quilt the project.
See page 74. I use the Trumpet Vine as an example of how to quilt these projects.

Add a hanging sleeve, bind the edges, and add a label.
See page 75.

Trumpet Vine leaves
Cut from green.

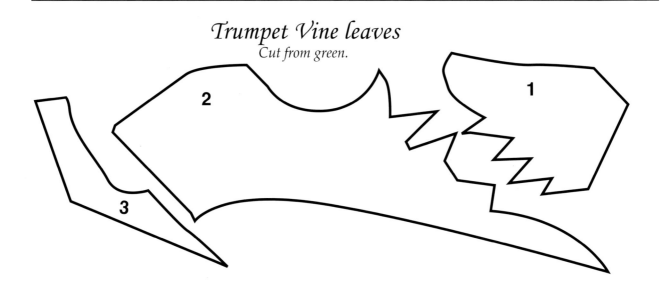

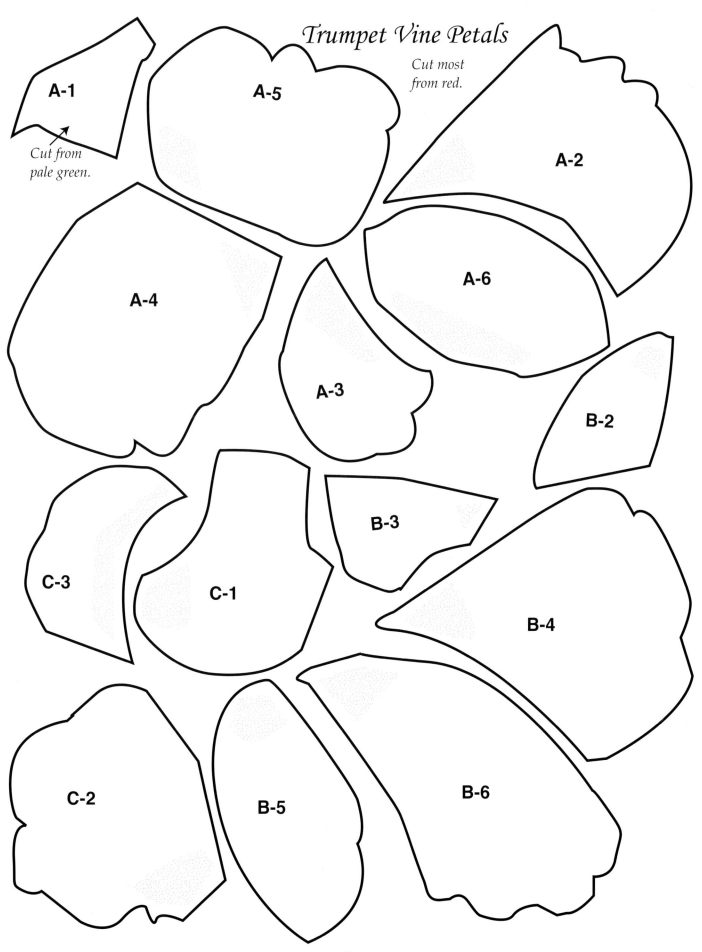

Trumpet Vine Petals

Cut most from red.

A-1

Cut from pale green.

A-5

A-2

A-4

A-6

A-3

B-2

B-3

C-3

C-1

B-4

C-2

B-5

B-6

Trumpet Vine Petals

Cut from red.

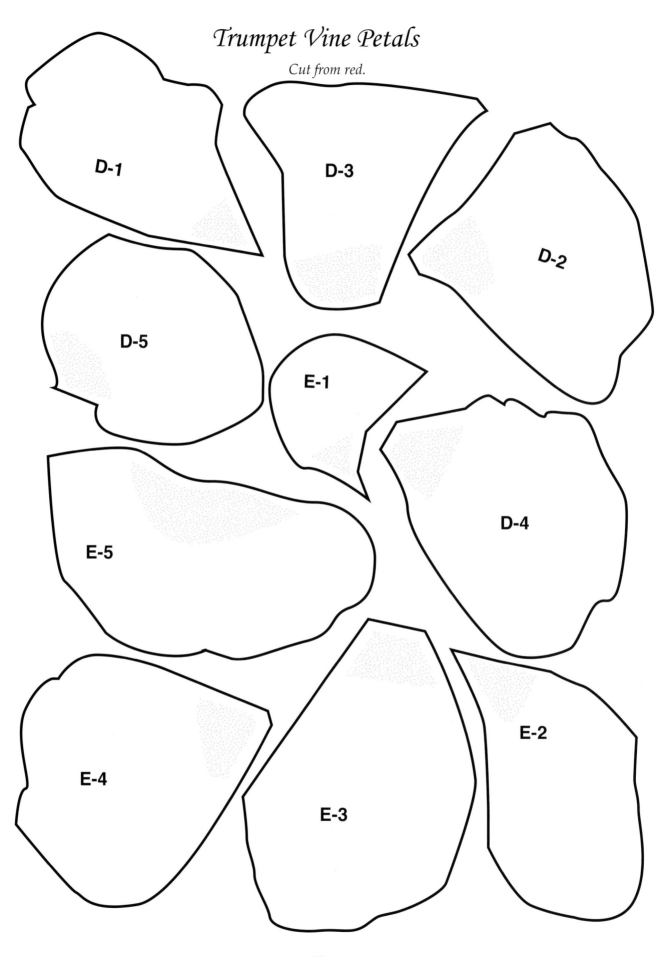

D-1

D-3

D-2

D-5

E-1

D-4

E-5

E-4

E-3

E-2

Trumpet Vines placement guide

Enlarge 200%.

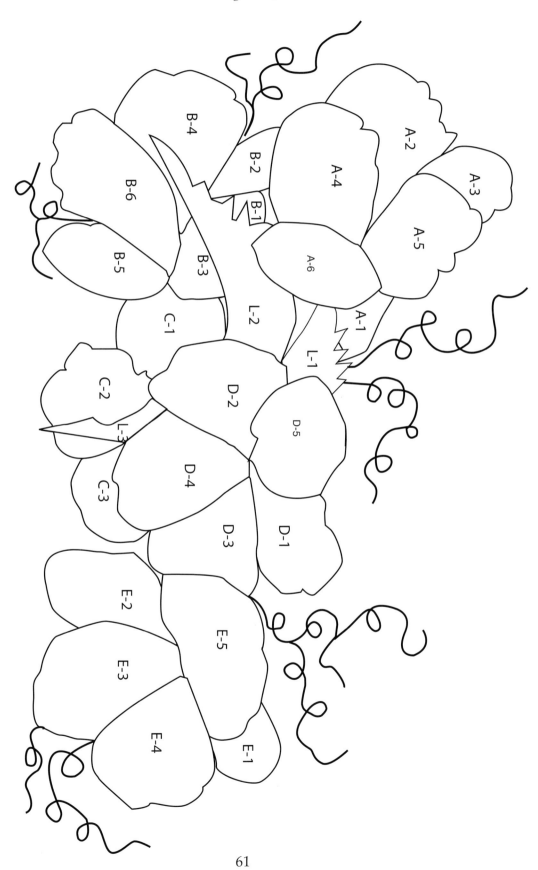

Tropical Hibiscus

We have had an hibiscus plant in our yard for many years because we liked having fresh tropical-looking flowers from early spring to late fall. When I found out that the hibiscus is the state flower of Hawaii, it was a natural addition to my floral pattern collection because we have a daughter-in law from Hawaii. In fact, she is waiting patiently to claim this quilt when I no longer need it for producing this book. Watch your loved ones try to claim your finished hibiscus quilt when they see the stunning color of the hibiscus flower.

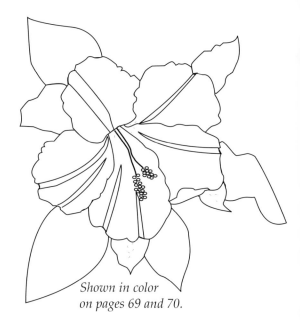

Shown in color on pages 69 and 70.

My flower is huge, as you'll see on page 69. I have adapted the instructions so you can make yours quite a bit smaller. Adjusted size with borders is about 25 " x 27" (1" inner border, 3" outer border).

Supplies for the smaller version

You will need the general supplies and tools listed on page 10, plus these supplies.

Fabric:
2/3 yard for background
1/2 yard of multi-color for flowers
1/8 yard or scraps of green
1/4 yard for the inner border
3/4 yard print fabric for outer border and binding
1 yard print fabric for backing
Batting about 29" x 31"

Steam-a-Seam2:
4 sheets

Hot Ribbon:
1 Red #2
1 Lemon Yellow #8
1 Maroon #9
1 Orange #13
2 Forest Green #14

Crystals (optional)
8 to 10 of each:
    #7 Citrine
    #10 Cosmo Jet
    #34 Sun
    #11 Crystal

Making Tropical Hibiscus

Create the design.
See pages 5-7. The shading is important in this design. Mark your pattern pieces so you can take advantage of the darker areas of fabric.

Embellish it with Hot Ribbon, crystals, and markers.
See pages 8-9, page 39, and pages 68-69.

Finish the quilt.
Add borders (pages 72-73). Quilt and bind it with your favorite methods, or see pages 74-75.

Tropical Hibiscus leaf pieces

*For smaller scale design. (Enlarge this page
160% on 11" x 17" paper for Giant Hibiscus.)*

Cut from green.

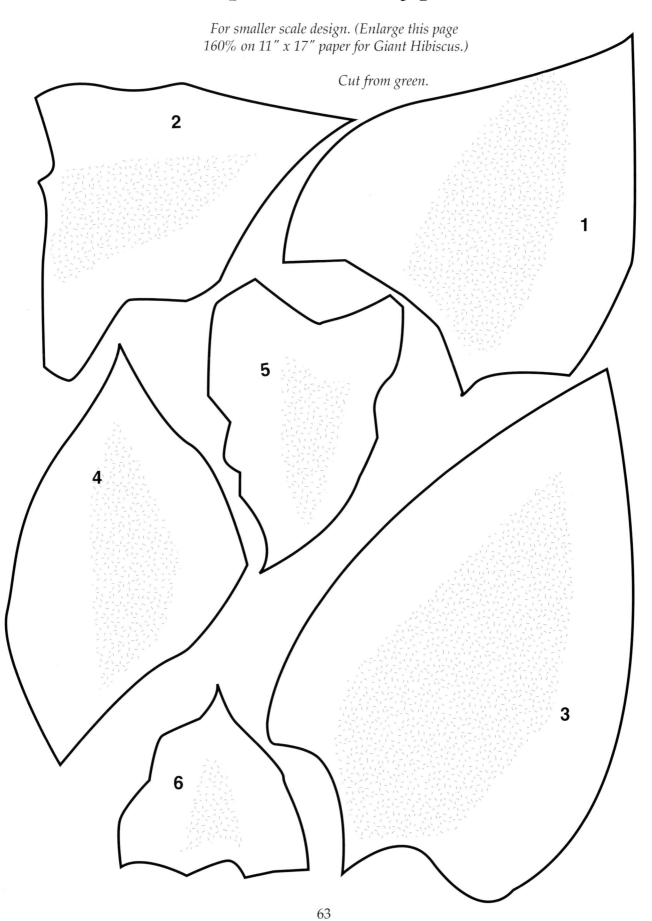

Tropical Hibiscus leaf pieces

For smaller scale design. (Enlarge this page 160% for Giant Hibiscus.)

Cut from green.

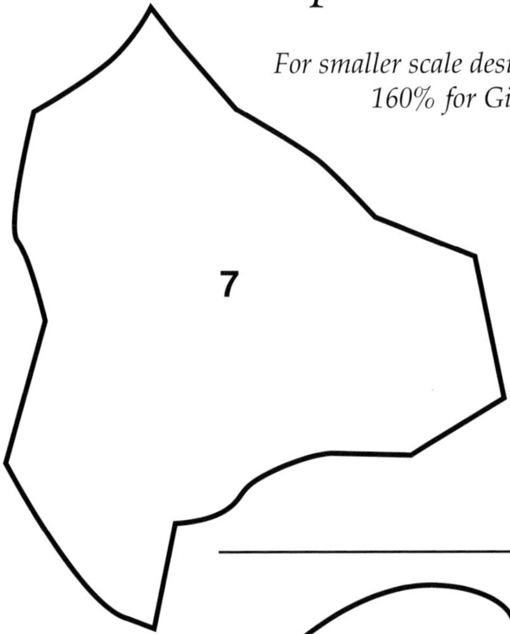

7

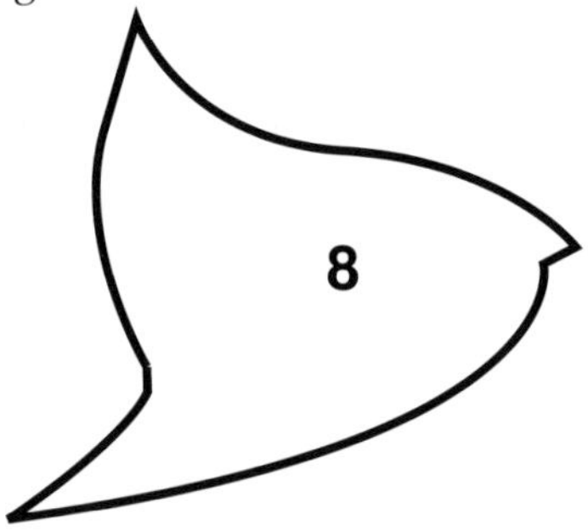

8

Petal pieces

Cut from orange.

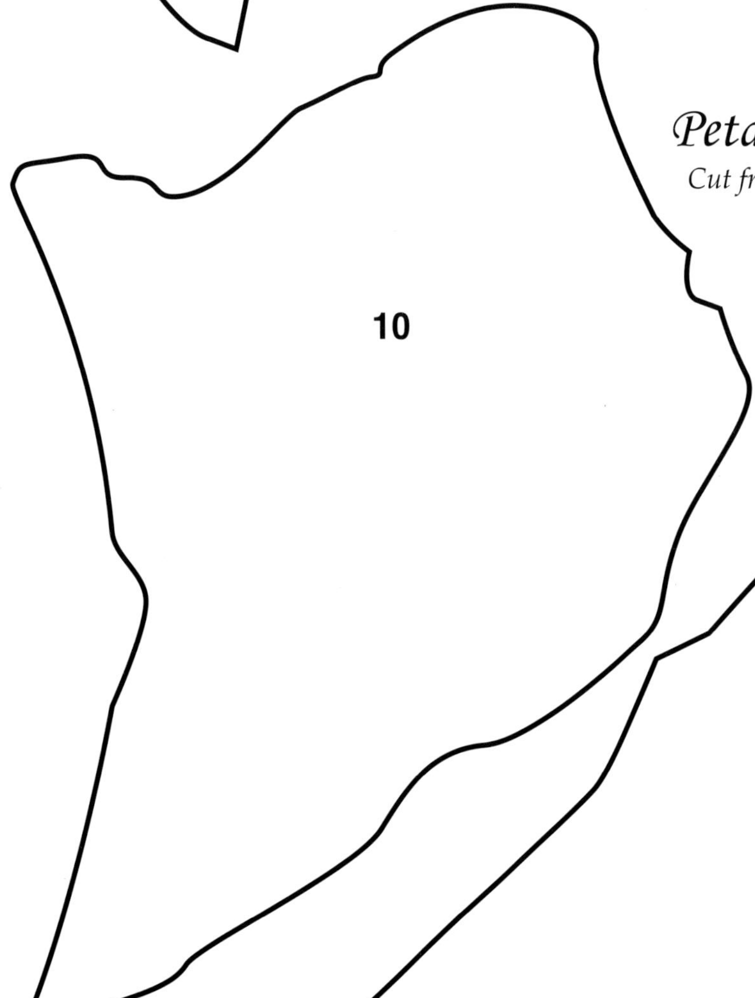

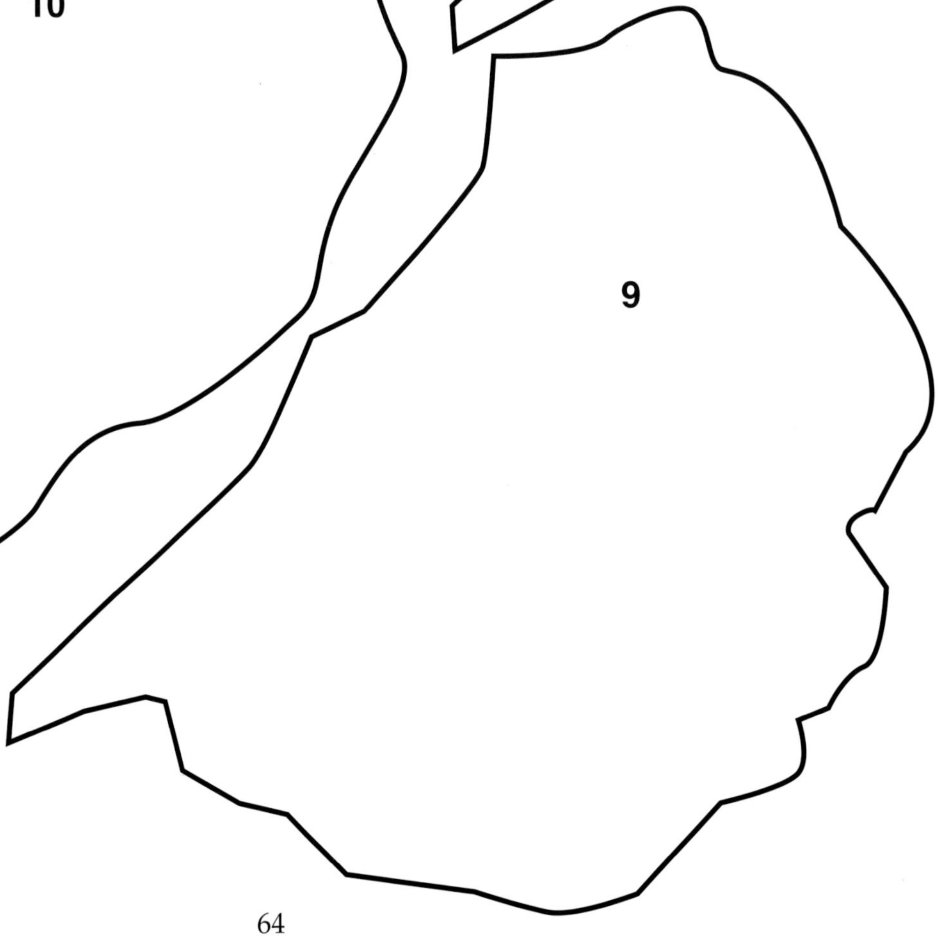

11

10

9

Tropical Hibiscus petal pieces

*For smaller scale design. (Enlarge this page
160% on 11" x 17" paper for Giant Hibiscus.)*

Cut from orange.

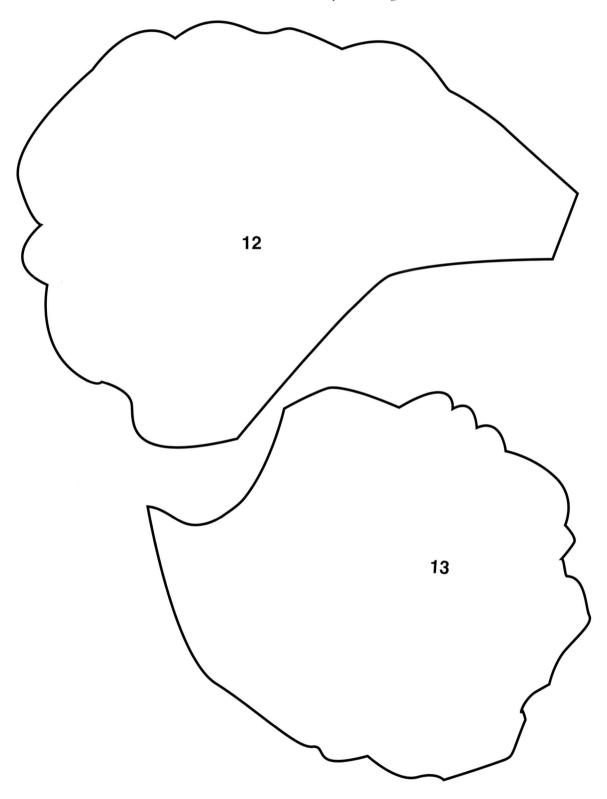

Tropical Hibiscus petal

*For smaller scale design. (Enlarge this page
160% on 11" x 17" paper for Giant Hibiscus.)*

Cut from orange.

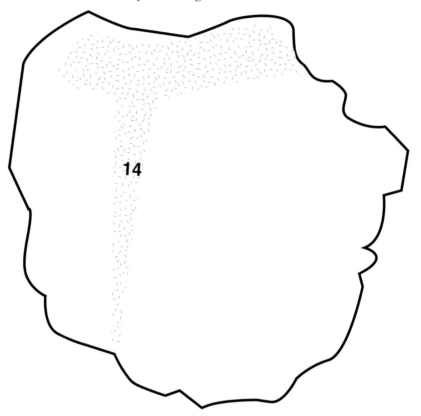

14

Stripes on the petals

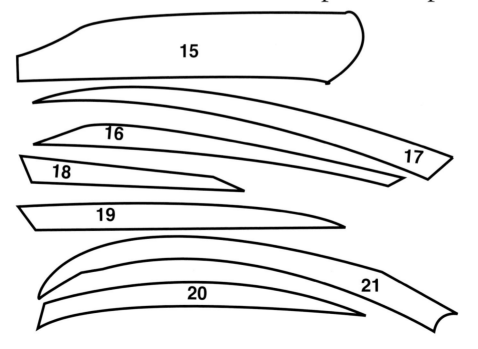

15

16

17

18

19

20

21

Tropical Hibiscus placement guide

Enlarge 200% (for the smaller scale project.)

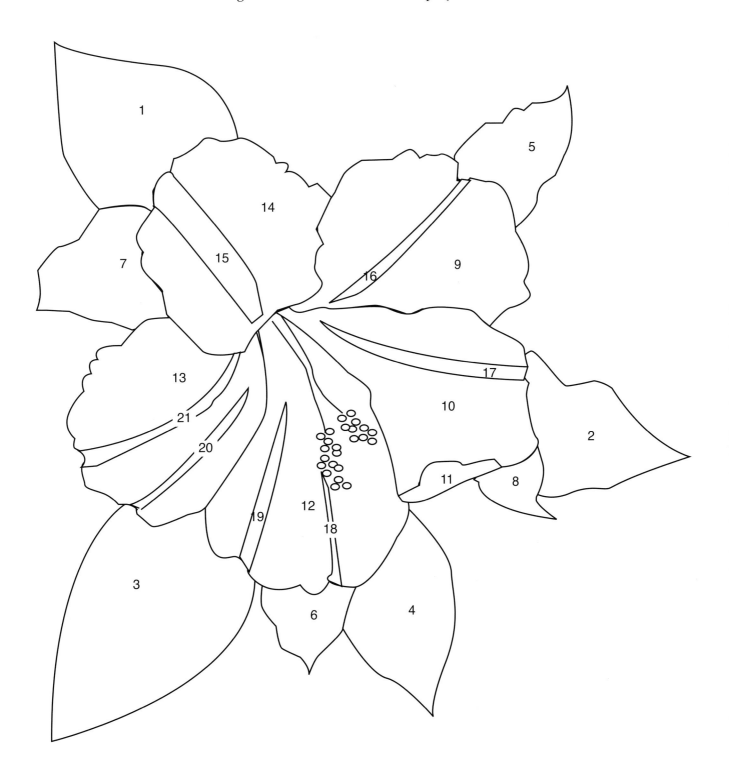

Adding crystals

Swarovski Crystals give a nice sparkle to the centers of the flowers. Here's how to apply them with a Bejeweler tool.

Preheat the Bejeweler.
Install a flat tip, not a concave one. (The concave tool gets too close to the fabric and might damage it.) Preheat the Bejeweler a few minutes.

Arrange your design on a hard, flat surface.

Pick up a crystal with tweezers.
Hold the tweezers in your right hand (unless, like me, you're left-handed). Make sure the glue side is down and place the crystal where you want it.

Apply heat.
Continue to hold the crystal while you pick up the application tool with your other hand. Place the tip directly on top of the crystal. See how I'm doing it in the photograph. Take the tweezers away, but hold the tool on the crystal for approximately 8 seconds for smaller crystals and about 12 seconds for the larger ones.

Continue applying crystals.

Test for bonding.
After the crystals cool, use your fingernail to check each one to see if it's on securely. If a crystal seems loose, apply heat again.

Care of the design.
If you need to press the fabric, use a dry iron and press it on the reverse. The project can be gently machine washed.

Safety precautions are the same as for the Clover Mini-iron.
- *Be careful not to touch the hot iron.*
- *Park it in a mug while you're using it.*
- *Keep it away from small children.*

Embellishing the Exotic Hibiscus

Here I am applying Swarovski Crystals with the Bejeweler. The mug I use for the mini-iron again comes in handy to park the hot tool.

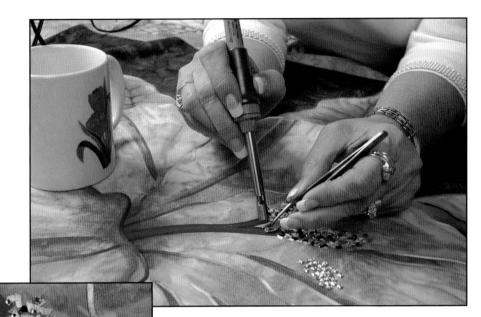

Here is the final result.

Along with the crystals I have used snippets of Hot Ribbon.

I usually add color and dimension to my projects with markers, especially in the centers. I can go back to add more shading at any time.

Note: My Hibiscus is very large. I've given you the option of making a smaller version.

Tropical Hibiscus

Project size with borders is about 25" x 27". Directions begin on page 62.

Using other appliqué methods

I realize that just as I love to do appliqué with Hot Ribbon, some of you prefer other techniques. Feel free to adapt these designs to your favorite methods.

Hand appliqué.

One thing I like about using Hot Ribbon with appliqué is that I can cut pieces the exact size I need. I don't have to measure the extra amount needed for turning under.

If you want to hand appliqué the patterns in this book, you will need to cut the pieces 1/8" larger on each side. This will give you just enough material for turning under and still have the pieces fit together.

Machine applique with satin stitching.

Another option for finishing the pattern is to use your sewing machine with either a satin stitch or a buttonhole stitch. With the satin stitch and the right thread color, you can give the appliqué a look similar to Hot Ribbon. Satin stitching takes a lot of practice and not everyone can do it accurately.

If you prefer the buttonhole stitch, I recommend using a neutral color thread to ensure that you do not detract from the pattern.

Share your creations.

If you try these designs with other appliqué methods, I'd love to see a photograph of your work and get your comments about how you did it. E-mail them to me at lennie@dutchquilter.com.

How to finish your quilt

How to add borders

I think these projects look best with a narrow inner border of solid color or variegated fabric. Sometimes I use two narrow borders, which repeat colors found in the design. Then I add a wider border, which might be a print fabric. Mitered corners are nice, but lapped corners are much easier, so that's what I'll give directions for.

Choose the fabrics.
See the opposite page. Look for fabrics that complement the design but don't overpower it.

Square up the design.
Measure through the middle and at each end. Trim as needed.

Add inner borders.
Side borders:
- Cut two strips the length of your quilt and 1-1/2" wide.
- Sew them to the sides of the design.
- Press the seams.

End borders:
- Measure the width, including the borders.
- Cut two strips that length and 1-1/2" wide.
- Sew them to the top and bottom of the design.
- Press.

Add outer borders.
Side borders:
- Measure the length, including the inner borders.
- Cut two strips that length and 3-1/2" to 4-1/2" wide.
- Sew them in place, and press as before.

End borders:
- Measure the width, including the borders.
- Cut two strips that length and your chosen width.
- Sew them to the top and bottom of the design. Press.

Choosing border fabrics

The best way to choose borders is to take your quilt to the fabric shop (or the room where you keep your stash) and try out many different fabrics. Lay out layers to represent the inner and outer borders.

Tip: Use a Polaroid or digital camera to take a picture of each good combination. Compare the results and choose the best.

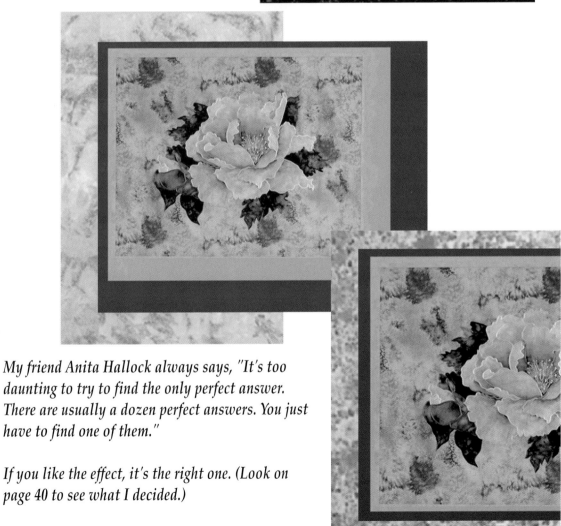

My friend Anita Hallock always says, "It's too daunting to try to find the only perfect answer. There are usually a dozen perfect answers. You just have to find one of them."

If you like the effect, it's the right one. (Look on page 40 to see what I decided.)

How to quilt the project

*Because of multiple layers of fabric and fusible web in some places, hand quilting would be difficult. It needs to be machine quilted. Here's a **good way to** do that important step.*

Get everything ready.

- Press the quilt top and square it up on all four sides. Remove all loose threads.
- Cut the batting at least 1" larger than the quilt top on each side. (If you're using a long-arm machine or quilting frame, have it 2 to 4" larger on each side.)
- Cut the backing the same size as the batting or a little larger.
- If you will be quilting with a small sewing machine, baste or pin layers together with medium size safety pins every few inches. (Stretch the design on the quilting frame if you have a long-arm machine.)

Quilt with a free-motion technique so you can outline shapes.

1. Start at the center and outline any small shapes where there is no design. Stitch right next to the ribbon outline, but try not to stitch over the ribbon.

2. Outline the whole cluster, again stitching near the ribbon. you might stitch over an occasional ribbon tendril, but that's okay.

3. Quilt a simple motif in the inner border.

4. Fill up the background with stippling (continuous curving lines meandering randomly).

5. Do more stippling in the outer border.

6. Do a small amount of quilting in the design area to help the project lie flat. Try to stitch lines that enhance the design.

How to add a sleeve

Since this is a wall quilt, you'll want to have a nice hanging sleeve.

1. Cut a wide strip.
   From the same fabric used for the backing cut a 9"
   strip as long as the top edge of the quilt. (Quilt
   shows usually require 4" finished sleeves.)

2. Stitch up the ends.
   Fold it with right sides together. Stitch up the ends
   about 1-1/2" from the edge of the quilt. Turn it
   right side out and press it.

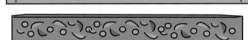

3. Sew it to the back of the quilt with a 1/4" seam.

4. Slip-stitch the folded edge to the quilt.
   The raw edge will be covered by the binding.

Invisible stitching

How to bind the edges

There are many ways to do binding, so use your favorite technique. I always get good marks from the quilt show judges with this method.

1. Spread out the quilt and trim it carefully.
   Square up the quilt exactly.

2. Make four strips.
   Cut strips 2-1/2" wide, the length of each side plus 2" on each end. I use straight strips because bias strips don't hold their shape. Fold each strip over, wrong sides together, and iron it.

3. Stitch them in place.
   Sew a doubled strip to each side, on the front of the quilt, with the raw edge 1/4" in from the edge of the quilt top. Start and stop 1/4" from the corner.

4. Miter the corners.
   Miter the corners by machine. (Practice this on pot-holder-size projects first.)

5. Fold the binding to the back and stitch it neatly by hand with a blind stitch.

How to add a label

Write with a indelible pen on a piece of fabric who made the quilt, when it was made, and what special significance it has. Sew to the back of the quilt.

Resources

All of these companies have web pages with dealer or mail order information.

Dutch Quilter - www.dutchquilter.com

This is my company. My e-mail address is lennie@dutchquilter.com. See pages 77-79 for information about my other publications. I also have some of the tools and supplies available by mail order.

Hoffman Fabrics - www.hoffmanfabrics.com

I can count on them for perfect fabrics for my floral designs. This company has generously supplied much of the fabric you see in this book.

Imagination International - www.hotribbon,com.

*This company in Eugene, Oregon, imports **Hot Ribbon** and **Copic Markers** from Japan. Call them toll free at (866) 662-6742. They have also been generous in providing supplies for me to experiment with.*

Cheri's Crystals - www.cheriscrystals.com

Cheri Meineke-Johnson imports Swarovski's Crystals from Austria. Contact her at 940-497-6399.

The Warm Company - www.warmcompany.com

*Based in Seattle, they have such great products as **Steam-a-Seam2** and **Soft & Bright batting.***

Bear Thread Designs - www.bearthreaddesigns.com

***Applique Pressing Sheets** are distributed by this company in Highland, Texas.*

All other sewing notions are available at most sewing shops, quilt shops, and mail order houses.

My first book

I live in California, but my favorite lighthouses are in Oregon. I published this book in 2005.

It uses the same techniques you have learned in Floral Fantasies, but projects are generally larger, about 35" x 40" with borders.

It has 64 pages, with eight pages of color photographs. Suggested retail price $19.95 plus $3.00 postage.

OREGON COAST LIGHTHOUSES

featuring

Hot Ribbon Appliqué

BY LENNIE HONCOOP

Projects in this book

1 • *Umpqua Lighthouse*
2 • *Cape Blanco Lighthouse*
3 • *Yaquina Lighthouse*
4 • *Coquille River Lighthouse*
5 • *Heceta Lighthouse*
6 • *Heceta Lighthouse Panorama*

More floral designs

If you didn't see your favorite flowers in this book, maybe you'll spot them here. Make them with the same no-sew technique given in this book. These individual patterns are $10.50 each.

TOP:

FS1 • *Elegant Iris*
FS2 • *Dutch Tulips*

MIDDLE:

FS3 • *Pansy Bouquet*
FS4 • *Golden Sunflower*

BOTTOM:

FS5 • *Regal Roses*
FS6 • *Festive Poinsettia*
FS7 • *Spring Daffodil*

Most designs are about 18" x 27" before borders, about 25" x 34" after borders.

Vineyard Designs

My Vineyard designs, printed in 2003 and 2004, are the first patterns ever published for Hot Ribbon appliqué—at least the first in English! $10.50 each.

VS 1 • Wine in a Glass

VS 2 • Wine in a Crock

VS 3 • Wine from Italy

VS 4 • Wine Country Retreat

Again, pattern sizes vary. Most are about 25" x 34" finished.

If your local quilt store does not carry my book and patterns, you can order them directly from me. Please include $1 postage for each pattern, $3.00 for each book. Send your check to:

Lennie Honcoop
4105 Saul Court
Elk Grove, CA 95758

Phone 916-683-1215
E-mail: Lennie@dutchquilter.com
web site: www.dutchquilter.com

Let me know if you would like your book or patterns autographed.